The Essentials of Beautiful Singing

A Three-Step Kinesthetic Approach

Karen Tillotson Bauer

THE SCARECROW PRESS, INC.

Lanham • Toronto • Plymouth, UK

2013

Published by Scarecrow Press, Inc.
A wholly owned subsidiary of The Rowman & Littlefield Publishing Group, Inc.
4501 Forbes Boulevard, Suite 200, Lanham, Maryland 20706
www.rowman.com

10 Thornbury Road, Plymouth PL6 7PP, United Kingdom

British Library Cataloguing in Publication Information Available

Library of Congress Cataloging-in-Publication Data

Bauer, Karen Tillotson.
  The essentials of beautiful singing : a three-step kinesthetic approach / Karen Tillotson Bauer.
      pages cm
  Includes index.
  ISBN 978-0-8108-8687-2 (cloth : alk. paper) — ISBN 978-0-8108-8688-9 (pbk. : alk. paper)
  — ISBN 978-0-8108-8689-6 (ebook) 1. Singing—Instruction and study. I. Title.
  MT820.B2846 2013
  783'.043—dc23
                                                                                            2013013994

Contents

Part III: Refinements toward Greater Skill

List of Figures

Acknowledgments

$\mathcal{I}$t takes a village. This is true for writing a book even though the actual writing is a solitary endeavor. It has been a labor of love, an outgrowth of my passion for singing and the teaching of singing. I am grateful for the opportunity to put into writing the essence of my work in the voice studio and in the classroom. Many supportive "villagers" in my life have ultimately floated this work into the book you now hold in your hands.

First of all, I extend my gratitude to Scarecrow Press for seeing the value in this book and for adding it to its list of publications. I am also grateful for its excellent senior editor, Bennett Graff, who has been a perpetual source of information over the last several months. The multitudinous questions I had were always answered with expertise, collegiality, and dispatch. It was clear to me from the start that I was fortunate to be in partnership with him.

I am indebted to North Park University, where I've taught for more than thirty years, for giving me the platform to live out my passion for teaching and for the sabbatical that provided me the space and time to begin this writing effort. As I had requested, I was allowed an extended time frame to teach half-time and write half-time. Teaching is a "doing" thing, both in the studio and in the classroom, whereas writing is a "talking" thing. Rather than retreating from teaching for a prolonged period to sit in front of a computer, I was able to experience the synergy of teaching and writing simultaneously. What I taught at school, I wrote in the book, and what I wrote about, I taught.

I am grateful to Stephen A. LaTour, whose book with coauthor Julia Davids, my colleague at North Park, had recently been published. Stephen graciously gave me a crash course on book publishing, giving fair warning about the enormity of the venture I was about to begin. After a few of those instructional sessions, my husband and I enjoyed an evening over dinner with Stephen and his wife, Pauline. At one point Pauline, who had been asking about the nature of the book, said, "Then this is a book you couldn't have written before now." I had never thought about it like that, but she was right; *this* book could not have been written until now. It has been brewing for a long time. If I had attempted a book thirty or even fifteen years ago, it would have been quite different from this one—shorter on experience and less quirky, for good or bad!

Several people were early readers of my beginning effort. It was important to run it by these esteemed colleagues and receive both their challenges and their affirmation.

The book became more real to me as I shared it with others. Craig Johnson, the new dean of the North Park University School of Music, was one of the first to read sections of it. It was incredibly generous of him to take the time in his first busy year at North Park to cheer on this phantom faculty member who, thanks to her sabbatical, only appeared on campus two days a week!

My long-time friend and colleague Wayland Rogers also came to the rescue. Wayland is an accomplished musician, singer, conductor, and well-published composer, so his expertise and perspective were valuable. I am grateful for his insightful comments. He has been in my "village" for many years, and I feel fortunate for having rubbed shoulders with such a talented musician.

Several years ago, I had the honor to work with Richard Dale Sjoerdsma, distinguished editor in chief of the *Journal of Singing* (from the National Association of Teachers of Singing) and professor emeritus at Carthage College. I had written two articles on the Baroque solo cantata that were accepted for the journal. I was impressed then with the depth and breadth of Dick's knowledge about music and singing. The grace and professionalism with which he continues his work on the journal are unmatched. He read some sections of my book early on, made some explicit and insightful comments, and gave me encouragement to forge ahead. That meant a lot to me.

The more I've gotten to know Kenneth Bozeman—Frank C. Shattuck Professor of Music and chair of the Voice Department at Lawrence University—the more I have come to regard him as a most enlightened teacher both in the applied art of teaching and in current voice research, including new technologies, especially in the science of acoustics. I look forward to his book that will be coming out soon. While Ken's research perspective is different from the perspective of this book, it is precisely because of that difference that his comments have been so valuable and interesting. He met my nontechnical style of writing with his technical perspective, and that made for a priceless interaction. He both challenged and affirmed, and I valued both. Ken not only read early sections but graciously continued to read the lion's share of the book and send comments on. I am appreciative of his willingness to share.

No one has shared more in this endeavor than my dear husband, Harold Bauer. He is now retired after a fifty-year career as conductor of orchestra and opera. If there is one thing that he might have wished to be besides a conductor, it would have been a singer. He loved his work with singers throughout the years. However, until becoming an astute reader of my book, he had never ventured much into the technique of singing. Lucky for me, he has a sharp editorial eye. Not only did he catch typos and less-than-clear sentences, but he tried out every exercise in the book! If he didn't understand how to do what I was suggesting, I rewrote it.

My children, Chris and Jennifer, are grown and on their own, but they had a little less of me throughout this writing process. I'm grateful for their understanding, interest, and patience throughout my writing endeavor. I'm particularly grateful for their occasional reminders to take some time out, advice I sometimes needed and heeded.

As I look over the landscape of my professional life, I can't help but think of the late Paul Kiesgen. He had been a friend since undergraduate days at Northwestern. We sang together, studied together, taught together, worked in the Chicago chapter of the National Association of Teachers of Singing together, and socialized with our families when we could. We kept in touch all those years up to a week before he died. I had often thought that I would write a book with Paul, but by the time I was "ready," his health was failing. I am grateful to have had Paul as a friend and to have observed his dogged commitment over the years to building a distinguished teaching career.

I am deeply grateful for the many students I've taught who brought with them not only their voices but their enthusiasm and passion for singing. I have been honored to help them find their voices both literally and metaphorically, often a life-altering process for them. This has energized me on a daily basis, and the countless relationships have provided much reward. One of the students, Cameron Scholtes, put a creative label to my teaching approach before it was an "official" approach. More on that in the overview (chapter 1).

My appreciation for what other pedagogues and voice scientists have shared in books or master classes is boundless, and if the goal of those efforts was to inspire learning how to sing and learning how to teach, it has been a job well done. The community of singers and teachers of singing, part of my extended "village," has given rise to many diverse methods for assimilating and teaching vocal techniques. The Three-Step Kinesthetic Approach is just one of those ways.

Introduction

This book is the product of many and diverse experiences I have had as a singer, voice teacher, classroom teacher, choral conductor, and opera director, mostly at the university level. For more than thirty years, working with soloists and choristers, from beginning students to emerging professionals, has given me a broad perspective on singers and their development. My classroom work in voice pedagogy and my studio work in private applied voice have interacted and enhanced each other with incredible synergy. My associations with professional colleagues in formal and informal settings have been meaningful in my development, and giving voice master classes has been an enriching part of my professional outreach. Although I've worn many hats in my teaching career, helping singers to develop their voices literally and metaphorically has been the primary focus and passion of my professional life.

These rich experiences, individually and aggregated, have morphed into the practical approach to singing described in this book. *The Essentials of Beautiful Singing: A Three-Step Kinesthetic Approach* is designed to lend simplicity to a complex task. From that perspective, it might shed new light on established principles of fine singing for the singer or teacher of singing and make it easier to apply those principles. Despite its intentional simplicity of style and content, I believe it is rooted in scientific discovery and well-tested traditions. The Three-Step Approach directly addresses the skills needed in the essential areas of breath management, resonance, and enunciation.

Over the years, I have been struck by the difference between the skills of a fine singer and those of a fine voice teacher. The skills are integrally connected, but they don't always come in the same person. To perform as a singer requires a skillful vocal technique and a sensitive musicality to sing convincingly and beautifully. The singer may or may not be able to articulate how he or she accomplishes that, let alone how to teach it to anyone else. Yet, a teacher must have a broad, objective understanding of the mechanics of technique to effectively teach a variety of students. At least as important as the knowledge base, especially in matters of physiology, is the manner of communicating it to the student. Effective communication must directly relate the scientific underpinnings of the functional singing voice to the singer's actual experience of it. It requires a terminology that speaks to the kinesthetic experience of singing, thus forming a bridge between fact and application. This has been a major motivator for me in my teaching and in writing this book.

Another motivator has been my growing awareness of how differently I approach the voice studio compared to the voice pedagogy class, in terms of teaching both style and content. Even though the two venues focus on the same subject matter—healthy, beautiful, and authoritative singing—they require different approaches.

Voice pedagogy courses primarily serve singers at the university level who want to become professionals as soloists, ensemble members, and choral directors, most of whom will teach voice at some point. To prepare singers for future teaching, it is absolutely necessary that they are offered a body of scientifically validated information covering the anatomy, physiology, and acoustics of singing, as well as the technologies associated with those studies.

In contrast, applied study must be primarily aimed at the creation of a beautiful voice in each singer who walks into the studio. For me, applied study calls for a terminology different from that of the classroom, one that more directly matches the mind–body connections that singers must make. Unlike the proven facts of scientific research, specific methods in the voice studio may (and should) vary from student to student.

Scientific inquiry has contributed much to the study of singing in both terminology and perspective, but singing requires its own unique mind-set and body awareness to activate correct functioning. It is a kinesthetic experience that becomes easier to assimilate if approached with clearly focused kinesthetic terms.

The Three-Step Approach addresses the physiology of singing with intentionally condensed explanations and guided exercises. The exercises combine specific physical preparations with rudimentary vocalizations. If approached mindfully, they can produce results that are anything but rudimentary.

With a focus on the physicality of singing, the approach has some built-in parameters beyond which it will not venture. With all due respect to the use of imagery, it will not play a role in the Three-Step Approach. Imagery can be too elusive and can lack the clarity that is a major goal of this particular approach. With even greater respect to scientific research, technical terminologies in the physiology and acoustics of fine singing will be utilized only as necessary, substituting simpler terminology whenever possible. Allow me to offer the reasons for these choices.

SCIENCE AND SINGING

Long before the enlightening scientific research of the twentieth century, most voice teachers taught with methods fashioned out of their own experience with singing, along with any natural teaching aptitudes they may have brought to the task. Such methods constituted an empirical approach to singing based on trial and error. They have their pitfalls to be sure, but almost any method can, including one that is well inspired by scientific research. I must say that I prefer the certainties that science offers, even though one doesn't need to throw out the empirical baby with the bath water, so to speak.

Effective voice teaching still benefits from the same aptitudes, sensitivities, and listening skills of the early successful teachers. However, the advantages of scientific discovery are surely there for the taking. For the serious student of voice, voice pedagogy classes give due attention to current voice science. Countless fine books offer a wealth of specific scientific information upon which pedagogies are built. A strong grounding in the science of voice is worth its weight in gold, especially if it can be channeled into a terminology and kinesthetic process that make learning how to sing simpler and more natural. This would be the best of both worlds for the aspiring singer.

While the science of voice rightly forms a substantial part of the pedagogy curriculum at the university level, there is often a chasm between assimilation of scientific detail and the application of it in singing or teaching singing. Skills of assimilation and application are not necessarily found in the same curriculum or the same person. This has never been made clearer to me than in the case of one graduate student who requested to take an exam in pedagogy in an attempt to test out of the first semester of the pedagogy class. He felt confident that he knew the material, and it turned out that he did. In fact, his exam was the most incredible regurgitation of the basic tenets of voice pedagogy that I've ever seen in writing from a student! I passed him out of the first semester, although somewhat reluctantly. I didn't see him again until the second semester of the year-long class. In that semester, the focus shifts a bit from scientific groundwork to more methodology and mentored clinical teaching. It was then that I discovered what a failure scientific knowledge was for this bright student in terms of his teaching and even his own singing. Science did not transfer into applied skill. I regretted passing him on and felt I had done him and his lab students a disservice. Since then, I have closed the loophole that allowed this to happen! Fortunately, the student was willing to learn and was able to absorb a good deal in the second semester as well as in the required second year of pedagogy coursework and clinical teaching.

This experience further confirmed my commitment to a terminology that speaks directly to the physicality required of good singing. The Three-Step Approach focuses on kinesthetic application, the practical and experiential work in the voice studio and practice room, supported by science as I believe it to be. My goal is not to summarize the many distinguished books on the science of singing but rather to detail one perspective, one kinesthetic approach to singing.

The teachers I have encountered over the years in workshops, master classes, and university voice departments are curious people who keep abreast of current research and pedagogic viewpoints. I believe that we all practice our art on the shoulders of those who have contributed so much in the way of voice research and pedagogy built on voice science. For those well-read singers/teachers, this book might not present any new scientific information. However, the approach might offer insight into a simpler way of looking at that information. Cultivated simplicity is the methodological style here, and the intent is to offer an approach that most aptly serves the needs of the singer in training.

We can't forget the many singers who are taking lessons as an avocation and will never step foot in a pedagogy class or read any scientific literature. These amateurs may sing in church choirs or community groups and value good singing, but they may not seek mastery. Nevertheless, conscientious teachers seek to elicit the most beautiful voice possible given the natural talents, commitment, work ethic, and personal goals of their students, whether or not they are professionally bound or equipped with scientific background. The underlying essentials of beautiful singing are applicable at all levels of singing.

I must mention that it has taken years for me to cultivate this simple approach and is certainly not where I began my journey. I first became hooked on the contribution of voice science many years ago when I discovered William Vennard's *Singing: The Mechanism and the Technic*. I read it three times, cover to cover. I was so excited by this monumental work of voice science that I wanted to share it with my undergraduate pedagogy students. I assigned it as the sole text. I cringe now at the thought, not because I have any less respect for this breakthrough work, but because the sheer amount of scientific detail completely overwhelmed the students in their introduction to voice pedagogy. (I changed to another text the following year, so I speak from a brief experience only. I have since heard of at least one instance where the Vennard book has been used successfully as a primary text.) For whatever reasons, my course certainly did not help the students see the forest for the trees, as I had planned. I hereby offer my apologies to those students wherever they are. In that class, with limited contact hours, concentrating on the Vennard book cut short the time that I could spend on the practical applications that are essential to the kinesthetic experience of singing. I have since found a more meaningful balance between science and methodology in those classes. Be assured that Vennard's book remains a "go-to" book for me and is still on the reference list for use in required research papers, in addition to more current works.

IMAGERY IN APPLIED VOICE TEACHING

The use of imagery can contribute to effective teaching. Metaphorical mental images are often suggested by teachers to evoke some desired result from the singer. Those images might be associated with sensations in the body—qualities of sound, moods, or any other imaginative suggestions. They are often colorful, as when one asks for a more "golden" or "velvety" tone when seeking a richer tone. There is nothing scientific about these words, but they might indeed elicit a richer tone. Such images require imagination to produce the desired technical results. By their nature, images require the singer to make the leap from imagining to producing. Some singers can do this, but many cannot. Because imagery is elusive and sometimes difficult to replicate, it might lack dependability, consistency, or specificity.

Imagery often describes a result rather than the cause, so it might be more meaningful *after* the desired effect has been experienced rather than as a vehicle for finding it. Also, imagery directives can give the wrong message. For example, the traditional directive to "place the voice in the mask" refers to a way of creating a sense of vibrations in the front of the face, particularly above the mouth. This is thought by many to be the sine qua non of a ringing tone. The imagery has been in use for centuries, so one can hardly dismiss it as useless. However, there is an inherent potential for misinterpretation. For instance, while it may be true that a singer feels sensations in the face when resonating well, directing the student to *place* the voice there, or anywhere, might result in spurious manipulation of the vocal tract in an effort to guide the voice to a certain place. It leads singers to believe that their sinuses are important resonators, which we know is not true. The Three-Step Approach seeks to *allow* the voice to find free resonance where it will be when the body is properly serving that goal. More on this in chapter 4, in which resonance is addressed.

Given the limitations of imagery, I nevertheless think that an apparently successful image must be associated with a specific physiological occurrence. I have always thought that it would make an interesting and challenging study to look for identifiable and consistent relationships between imagery and physiology. It would require the resources of a well-equipped voice research lab and much clinical work.

Finally, I'd like to offer an anecdote that is just one perspective on the limitations of imagery, especially when used as the primary method for professionally bound singers. Years ago, I heard a young singer in a lead role at the English National Opera in London and was impressed with her performance. Later, I had the good fortune of chatting with her over dinner. We had studied with the same teacher in London, so, of course, we talked technique. What concerned her most was her inability to sing well when the voice was just not working right on a given day. If she woke up on a "good day," her voice was beautiful and easy. That's the voice I had heard that evening. But if she woke up on a day that was not a good day voice-wise, she didn't know what to do about it. She had been taught primarily with imagery, which for her was elusive, sometimes working and sometimes not. She felt that the lack of specificity and clear direction was the primary obstacle to a dependable technique and upward mobility in her opera career. Unfortunately, I don't know what became of her—and just possibly this says something.

That conversation stayed with me, and I have seen many examples of this perplexing situation over the years. It has been just one of many motivators for me to find better methods of communicating vocal technique. It's not that I shy away from all imagery, but it is beyond the focus of the Three-Step Approach.

*   *   *

My hope is that singers and teachers at all stages of development will find the book's practical approach to be a valuable tool in their work. I hope that it is clear that it is centered on universal essentials of fine singing and is broader than an idiosyncratic ideology or inflexible "method." Its clarifying perspective, terminology, and exercises with matching verbal prompts can meld with almost any traditionally sound method. The simplicity of style and content is designed to present a clear view of the singer's forest through the trees, so to speak.

Because the approach does not require a sophisticated knowledge base or terminology, it is user-friendly for the amateur as well as the professionally bound singer. It can be used concurrently with private lessons or voice pedagogy class, or it can be used independently. The concrete ideas, mostly in the form of physical directives, clarify the physical processes of making beautiful tones. Of course, working with a good teacher who resonates with this approach (excuse the pun) would be even better.

I believe that the approach can augment, clarify, and reinforce the instruction of many voice teachers as well as choral directors.

Just as I have learned to focus my work better in the pedagogy class, my work in the voice studio over the years has evolved into the focused simplicity with which I speak in this book. In my experience, I have found that, sometimes, less is more.

Despite my scientific underpinnings, I have always thought that the art of teaching is more in the doing of it than in the talking about it. It is odd, indeed, that I am now talking about it in the form of a book! However, as much as possible, this book is certainly a "doing book." This is explained more in the overview of the Three-Step Approach. For me, the challenge in writing the book has been to somehow capture in narrative form the spontaneous and interactive work experienced in the voice studio.

I have had ample evidence that students are able to retain the gist of this approach even years after having worked with it, if only in a brief master class. This is, I believe, because of its utter clarity and simplicity. Too often, master classes seem to work magic, but when the student goes into the practice room, replicating the magic is not possible. This book is not about voodoo but the simplest, concrete, physical realities of singing.

Part I gives an overview of the Three-Step Approach. It should help the reader get in touch with the big picture before focusing on individual steps. Following that, in preparation for the Three Steps, proper posture is addressed as a precondition of fine singing. Part II offers the details of the Three-Step Approach, one step at a time, chapter by chapter. Each chapter gives clear explanations of the process under discussion, along with exercises for facilitating the skill involved. Each chapter employs a short verbal prompt used as a focal point and snapshot reminder of explanations and exercises. Part III focuses on how the Three Steps can be broadened and finessed to refine the voice toward greater skill.

The essentials of beautiful singing—skilled breath management, resonance, and enunciation—form the backbone of the Three-Step Approach. The corresponding verbal prompts offer touch points for addressing those essentials as simply and clearly as possible.

Part I

SETTING THE STAGE FOR THE THREE-STEP APPROACH

Overview of the Three-Step Approach

$\mathcal{B}$efore detailing the work of the Three-Step Kinesthetic Approach, this overview offers a look at the big picture. It sheds light on the whole journey, what the parts are, and how they relate to an integrated vocal technique. The details of application come in subsequent chapters through the lens of a kinesthetic perspective, terminology, and exercises.

In no way minimizing the importance of voice science, concepts of vocal technique are applicable only if connected to the kinesthetic experience of singing, an experience of physical awareness and control. The Three-Step Approach is based on the premise that the process of learning how to sing would benefit greatly from a terminology that is in close relationship to the language and sensations of the body. It seeks to foster the kinesthetic intelligence that enables fine singing.

The Three-Step Approach is a distillation of the contributions of science and pedagogic experience. Its terminology simply reframes the underlying but often complex principles of fine singing to give them greater clarity experientially. It can avert or correct improper applications that are the result of misunderstandings.

In the acknowledgments, I mention the important role that students have played in the development of this approach. One of them, Cameron, was living abroad at the time and sent me an e-mail as an update on her comings and goings. She signed off, "Happy OOFing!" I had no idea what she meant until I scrolled down a bit to see her explanation. "OOFing" was her acronym for the repeated directives that she had heard from me during our work together: Open Body, Open Throat, Forward Articulation—*OOFing*. It brought a smile to my face, and I had to admit—it was an apt labeling of those short verbal prompts. This book, then, is a step-by-step venture into OOFing.

Exercises for the Open Body and the accompanying guidelines are designed to elicit the experience of an expanded body of breath, how it is created, how it feels, how it functions, and how it is maintained. Likewise, the exercises for the Open Throat are designed to elicit the experience of open, receptive resonating cavities and to demonstrate how they are created, maintained, and function with consistency. Exercises for Forward Articulation are designed to elicit correct movements of the articulators that make the text clear without impinging on the flexible Open Throat and the resonance enabled there.

The OOFing prompts are based on the science of voice as I have absorbed it over the years, but they reflect intentional simplicity of both style and terminology. The three simple physical directives focus on breath management, full resonance, and free enunciation: Open Body, Open Throat, and Forward Articulation, respectively. They are not the totality of the approach but are indicative of the nature of it. The prompts are mere reminders of the preparatory explanations given at the beginning of each chapter. They can be recalled in a moment's time without cluttering the thought process unnecessarily. Each prompt speaks directly to the specific physicality required of a particular task. Because the prompts are easy for the singer to internalize and recall, they can serve as familiar guideposts in forming a technique, correcting it, refining it, and maintaining it. They give focused structure to the practice room routine.

The prompts help the singer stay focused on the causative factors of fine singing as much or more than the tonal product. Singers often focus primarily on the tone as if it were an independent agent rather than the result of a well-integrated musical instrument. The OOFing mantra, a hallmark of the Three-Step Approach, can provide focus for singers at any stage of development.

By approaching the art of singing in practical, kinesthetic terms, this book might be regarded as an accessible manual of instruction for beautiful singing. As noted in the introduction, it is a "doing book," and this is very evident in the exercises offered and the accompanying guidelines. The exercises are relatively few in number and seemingly very simple. They are designed to facilitate body awareness and muscle memory in all parts of the singing instrument, be it for good breath management, resonance, or enunciation. The exercises are first prepared with condensed and clear explanations of the physical functioning that will be required to achieve meaningful success with them.

While most of the exercises involve sung tones, some do not. Some simply prepare the body to do its work. In all cases, though, the focus is on meeting the kinesthetic requirements of singing well. The correct physicality will produce the correct result.

The primary effort and focus of the exercises are on the physical preparation and continuing service to the tone. The vocalizations serve as a measurement of how effectively the body is working; if the body is working well, the tone will be good.

The vocalizations are not comprehensive, nor are they elaborate. They are mini-versions of more complex vocalises that singers often practice. Unfortunately, there are no vocalises per se that enable singers to sing well. Without the Open Body–Open Throat–Forward Articulation unit, they are of limited value. The premise in this approach is that the *body* improves the technique more than the vocalise.

By integrating seemingly simple vocalizations into a total kinesthetic experience, the singer can develop skills that easily transfer to more complex musical situations. This is borne out in part III, where refinements and higher levels of skill are explored.

The surface simplicity of the approach should not be interpreted as being solely for the beginner. While it can create a vocal technique where none has previously existed, it can just as well improve the technique of an advanced singer. In a trained voice, it can facilitate greater finesse and refinement or eliminate bad habits that inhibit further growth and development. The essentials of beautiful singing are essential at all levels.

Bad habits cause glitches in the voice. Most of them are caused by misunderstandings of one or more basic processes and therefore result in improper application of the underlying principles. This ultimately runs into dead ends. Often, singers consciously or unconsciously resort to camouflaging the glitches rather than addressing their causes. This is a short-term fix and an imperfect one. Even with very smart singers who possess wonderful vocal instruments, if the basic elements of good vocal technique are not addressed correctly, the singer's development will be continually limited.

In some ways, the Three-Step Approach mirrors the manner in which one's native language is learned. Children learn to speak before the superimposition of grammar and structure. More and more, language study centers are using the same approach for teaching adults, starting with the sounds rather than with the book. Similarly, singers can learn to sing before they have full comprehension of the science of singing. However, the more the student understands good singing in a kinesthetic sense, the more it will be repeatable with or without the teacher. This develops kinesthetic intelligence and, with it, greater potential for dependability.

A kinesthetic approach to singing might be compared to the approach of a good physical therapist. A trained therapist knows the body's physiology and how to mend dysfunctional members of the anatomy, but relevant physical exercises with clear explanations are necessary to elicit good functionality from the patients. Singers must functionally train their bodies, and in so doing, they will train their voices.

The well-studied voice teacher or advanced singer will no doubt mentally substitute more technical terminology as she or he reads through the book, and that is to be expected and appreciated. The term *Open Body* may elicit thoughts of the diaphragm, the abdominal muscles, and the external intercostals. The term *Open Throat* suggests the pharynx, the oral cavity, questions of light and dark, the singer's formant, nasality, placement, and constrictor muscles. The term *Forward Articulation* suggests clear enunciation, correct positions of the tongue, differences between consonants and vowels, and so on and so forth. However, as much as possible, this book gives the starring role to the three basic OOFing steps, for without those basic elements of singing—no matter what they are called—no technique or method can be entirely successful.

Before beginning specific work on the Three Steps, the issue of posture must be addressed. Good posture is fundamentally a matter of general physical fitness not to be reserved solely for singing. However, for the singer, exemplary posture is a precondition of fine singing. It is necessary for achieving success with the Open Body, Open Throat, and Forward Articulation. Therefore, it is addressed in the next chapter before moving on to the Three Steps in part II.

Part II approaches each step, one at a time. Separate chapters are allotted to the Open Body (breath management), Open Throat (resonance), and Forward Articulation (enunciation). The underlying premise of each verbal prompt is explained to provide context for the exercises that follow. Building on that, the guidelines for executing each exercise are designed to foster the appropriate kinesthetic experience. One step is methodically layered onto and integrated with the next, and ultimately, the Three Steps become an interdependent whole.

Part III addresses various refinements of vocal technique as it moves toward greater skill development. The same Three Steps that are detailed in part II—Open

Body, Open Throat, Forward Articulation—are broadened and finessed to facilitate skills involving issues of registration, the upper range, and *legato* singing.

Students are prone to falling into vocal "traps" while on the training path. This is only natural. In each chapter, the most common traps are noted as they relate to the particular vocal process under discussion, be it posture, breath management, resonance, or enunciation. Calling attention to the common traps should help the singer recognize or avoid them.

The discussions of traps automatically touch on the complexities of teaching singing and learning how to sing. It is all too common for singers to get hung up on minutiae of "methods," "feelings," "imageries," or "placement" and lose their primary mind–body connection. They forget the relative simplicity of the kinesthetic experience. They lose sight of the forest for the trees. The frustration that comes from this loss of focus is counterproductive and often unnecessary. The Three-Step Approach can serve as a homing device to guide the singer toward more simplicity of thought, approach, and physicality.

Phonation, the utterance of sound, is not presented as a separate process in this book, although it is unquestionably an essential element of voice physiology. It occurs in the larynx at the vocal folds. (Often, you will hear the folds referred to as *vocal cords*, but they are more accurately described as *folds*.) The folds and surrounding area are completely invisible to the naked eye and primarily respond reflexively rather than through direct conscious control. To stay focused on processes that can be consciously controlled, phonation is addressed only as it is integrated with the Three Steps. If those steps are working properly and if the vocal instrument is healthy, good phonation will respond quite naturally. It will be grounded in good breath management, enhanced with good resonance, and formed into understandable words with good enunciation. If the voice is not healthy, certainly the Three Steps may help, but medical supervision should be explored.

Although the Three-Step Approach is predicated on kinesthetic experience aided by simplicity of terminology, I am not implying that learning to sing beautifully is easy! However, I think much of the difficulty comes with what "issues" the singer brings to the table. (I don't allow the use of the word "problems" in my studio, only "issues.") The issues might present themselves in posture, tonal concept, muscle tonus, personality, or psyche. Breaking bad habits is usually more difficult than building new correct habits. This is where the good teacher will use his or her expertise and objective perspective to assess the singer's issues and determine how to resolve them.

While the role of the teacher is certainly important, singers becoming familiar with the Three-Step Approach could reasonably analyze the state of their vocal development even if they are not currently taking lessons. The exercises are clearly explained, and the perspective is as important as the details. Although the language and exercises seem simple, I believe there is a density of food for thought. Therefore, although the book may appear to be an easy read, I urge the reader to move through it slowly and mindfully. The singer would do best to read only one chapter at a time while experimenting with the exercises suggested in it.

The Three-Step Approach to singing is a humble one, grounded in simplicity as it is. However, as the reader can tell, I am a believer that the approach, while not the whole picture, is surely aligned with traditionally sound, healthy methodologies. While it has a particular slant, logic, and order, it should not be regarded as a "canned" method. Ideas can easily be extracted and used with other approaches. This would be natural for inquiring and curious voice teachers, most of whom are instinctive gatherers of pedagogical ideas.

The Three-Step Approach can be expanded in as many and diverse ways as there are teachers and singers. However, it is based on the undeniable essentials of beautiful singing, good breath management, resonance, and enunciation. They are approached with a simple kinesthetic terminology that can be easily recalled and that minimizes the risk of misunderstandings, manipulations, and other spurious singing efforts.

Enough talk! Now on to a discussion of posture as a precondition of good singing technique. Only after that discussion can we move on to some OOFing.

Posture: A Precondition of Beautiful Singing

As important as good posture is for good vocal technique, its value goes far beyond that. Good posture is an essential ingredient of healthy living. Methods for achieving proper body alignment are many and include overall physical conditioning, yoga training, and an approach called the Alexander technique. The advantages of a fit body with good posture are not exclusive to musicians. Because of the universal application and benefits of good posture, the subject is presented here as a precondition of beautiful singing rather than as one of the Three Steps that focus specifically on singing. These are addressed in chapters 3–5, but they can be effective only if the body is in a state of readiness through proper alignment.

CONTEXT

When unnecessary constrictions result in needless wear and tear on body parts, singers and instrumentalists alike may experience the debilitating results of a body that is not aligned. This can cause problems for musicians be they in the singer's voice, the cellist's shoulder, the violinist's neck, or any other body part that is not functioning optimally. Appropriate physical training, which includes correcting the posture, plays an important role in addressing such problems.

Good musicians must be functionally in harmony with their instruments to give technique and musicality every advantage possible. The art of singing is either helped by the body or hindered by it. In an aligned body, the muscular system supports the skeleton and makes all movement, activity, and workload freer, easier, and more efficient. The benefits of this are as applicable to singing or playing a musical instrument as they are to athletics or dance. Although the goals are different for these pursuits, they each require fine physical coordination to accomplish extraordinary things that are beyond "natural." It is no more natural to sing an aria beautifully with a full, free resonant voice than it is for the athlete to jump seven feet high or for the ballet dancer to do a beautifully executed pirouette. Good posture might not be quite as difficult to attain, but good health and well-being—and, certainly, good singing—require mindful focus on body alignment.

Although the body is naturally designed for good posture, achieving good posture may not seem so natural. It is a kinesthetic experience that may have become more habitual than thoughtful, more lax than energized. Because the skill of fine singing requires a finessed use of the body, posture must be equally finessed to serve the needs of good vocal technique. This chapter suggests an approach to posture that is, of necessity, more mindful than habitual, more energized than lax.

Gravity actively resists good posture, so it must be met with equally active energy in the lift of the body. Without it, the body succumbs to gravity, resulting in poor posture. This is evident in young people as well as aging people. It always gets worse with time if not corrected. Poor posture might be manifested in a collapsed chest, rounded shoulders, swayed back, lowered head, or any other misaligned body part, any of which will negatively affect the singing voice.

I have found that many students think that good posture is achieved by raising the chest and pulling back the shoulders. While there may be a need to lift the chest (if it is sunken) or pull back the shoulders (if they are rolling forward), this limited perspective misses the point of total body alignment. One needs to address the whole body, from the abdominal core to the spinal column—not just the chest or shoulders.

The alignment and balance of the skull are major players in good posture and often seem to be unnatural to singers. The spinal column is the body's central support extending well into the head. The head must be poised on top of the spine as if it would stay there even if it were not attached, perfectly balanced on its central pivotal point. Like many other teachers, I suggest to my students that they imagine their heads as those little bobble heads in the rear windows of cars, merrily and loosely balancing on the central support. In this position, the head is balanced and free to move as needed.

If the head is too far forward (most common), back, or to the side, it is out of balance and will constrict the throat. This affects phonation and resonance. A balanced head, like the proud lift of a ballerina's head, has the least effective weight and therefore requires the least work to maintain its position. The well-lifted and well-balanced head, with eyes looking straight ahead, gives the body a sense of weightlessness and readiness.

Some singers find the central balanced position of the head not only unnatural but even a little arrogant, particularly if the head has been too far forward. To the observer, though, it just gives the appearance of an energetic, alert, and buoyant person. It takes work to achieve this, but it is the kind of work that bodies are equipped for, work that frees rather than constricts.

Good posture is the active lift of the upper body—the thorax—and includes a spinal stretch. It creates an experience of height that allows the chest and shoulders to *fall* into place, without conscious manipulation of them. Such a stretch makes more room for the internal organs in the abdominal cavity and allows independence of the body's moving parts. It can easily add an extra inch or more to the overall height of the singer.

In figure 2.1, the body image on the left shows correct body alignment. The back of the head, upper back, and buttocks all touch the wall. The ears, shoulders, hip bones, and knees line up as if a straight vertical line could be drawn through them,

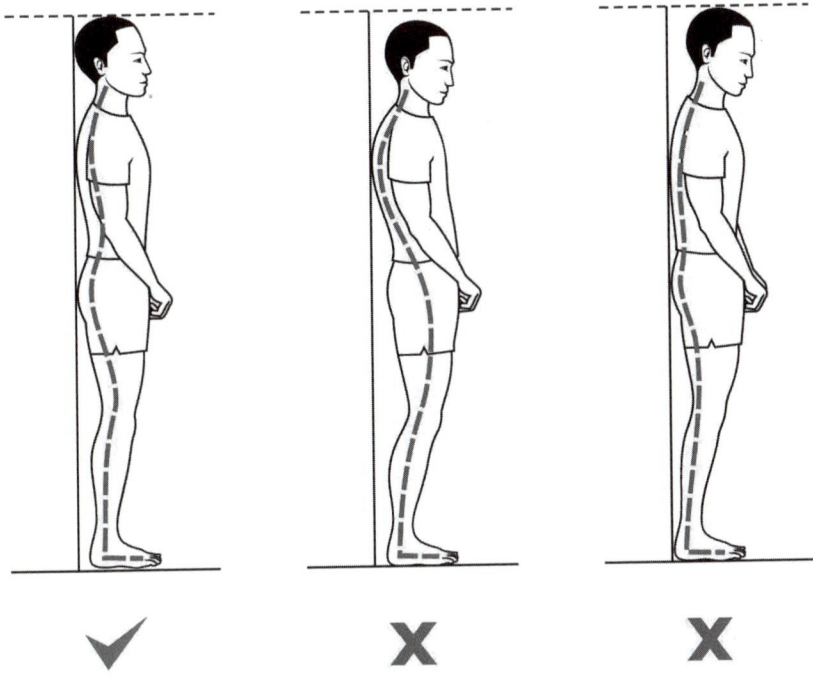

Figure 2.1.   Postural alignment.

even as the spine retains its natural, balanced curve shown by broken lines. The body is erect at full height, with a head position well balanced on the top of the spine.

The center image might be the most common type of misalignment. The head is forward and chin down, constricting the throat area. The shoulders roll forward, decreasing the possibility for chest or rib expansion. The upper torso seems to be merely sitting on the lower torso, which is one of the reasons that the body lacks height. Because the buttocks do not touch the wall and the pelvis is thrust forward, vertical alignment of ear, shoulder, hip, and knee is prevented.

The image on the far right of figure 2.1 appears to be the same height as the image on the far left. However, the body on the right achieves this with the crown of the head rather than the top of the head. This means that the head is rotated downward even more than the center image. A forward bend at waist level causes the chest to lower and the shoulders to roll forward, causing constriction in the abdominal cavity. The small of the back is pushed against the wall, thereby reducing the natural curve of the spine and taking it out of balance. It is apparent that this body is without energy and lacks the readiness needed for exercise of any kind.

Correct body alignment such as the left image in figure 2.1 can be accomplished only with an energetic stretch of the total body, the spine being a central element of that stretch. The singer is often quite surprised at how much energy it takes to achieve this state of stretch. Although habitual posture may be inadequate, it may feel more natural just because it is more familiar. To maintain the stretch requires continuous work in the body but becomes easier as strength is developed.

ACHIEVING BODY ALIGNMENT

Earlier I noted that this is a "doing" book and that exercises would be suggested to elicit the correct kinesthetic experience for whatever task is being addressed. The following exercise is the first of those and is offered as an aid for experiencing proper body alignment. It is similar to many such exercises using a wall as a checkpoint, ones that I used as a young singer and that many of my students have experienced at some point in earlier training. Specific guidelines for executing this and other exercises are marked with bullets. My hope is that this version of the exercise may elicit still more body awareness and trick the body into a state of good posture.

EXERCISE

- Stand against a wall, with your heels just a few inches from it.
- Tip your head back so its crown is touching the wall. You have to do a bit of a back bend to achieve this position, and it rightly feels awkward. This is not the end product, but for some reason, singers tend to achieve a better stretch beginning in this strange position. It's worth a try!
- Slide your head up the wall pulling your whole body up with it. Maintain head contact with the wall, but the point of contact will gradually change from the crown to the back of the head, due to the head's forward rotation as it pulls up. When you get to a position where you feel that your spine is stretched, your abdominal area broadened, and your height increased, check to see that you are in a similar position as the far-left image in figure 2.1. In this upright position, eyes looking straight ahead, you will be on your way to proper alignment.

Even though the core is probably well energized at this point, there is one more element that needs to be introduced before alignment is achieved. Unless your posture is similar to the image on the right in figure 2.1, with the small of the back pressing against the wall, it might still be swayed more than is natural and healthy. While there is normally a small concave curve here, it is often much too pronounced, and this negatively affects the singer's breathing.

- To lessen the degree of the curve, simply slide a hand into the negative space between your back waist area and the wall and try to minimize that space. You should not try to eliminate it totally. Although you may not realize this, you will be engaging the lower abdominal muscles (between the waist and pelvic bone) to do this. Engaging the abs in this way pulls the pelvis forward, thereby minimizing the sway back and bringing the body into vertical alignment, as shown in the image on the left in figure 2.1. The knees should be flexible, neither bent nor hyperextended. (Hyperextended legs, with knees pushed back as far as they can go, tend to increase the sway in the small of the back, making vertical alignment difficult if not impossible.)

From the front point of view, body alignment is evident when the horizontal line of shoulders and hips is parallel to the floor. The head should be not tipping to one side or the other but should be vertically aligned with the center of the body. Various tensions caused by tight, contracted muscles can cause a shoulder to lift or the neck to bend to one side. This must be avoided. Working in front of a mirror would be helpful. The energized body in alignment can be achieved and maintained while the head, neck, and arms are perfectly relaxed and free to move.

COMBINING THE EFFORT WITH MOVEMENT

It's one thing to find proper body alignment while standing against the wall and focusing on what the body needs to do. I sometimes have students sing entire songs at the wall. However, it's another thing to move away from the wall while maintaining posture that may not feel natural and to actually perform functions freely without the wall as a checkpoint. Maintaining the spinal stretch with abdominals engaged while at the same time moving body limbs freely can be a bit like rubbing your tummy and patting your head at the same time!

EXERCISE

- After achieving proper body alignment against the wall, walk away from it, maintaining the energetic spinal stretch that gives you added height along with the core engagement of the abdominals that pulls the pelvic area forward. Keep the head loosely balanced on top of your spine.
- Swing the arms and move the head as you walk. The arms should not have any tension in them and should be free to dangle from their sockets and move into any position without disturbing the torso's lift. Like the bobble head in the back of cars, your head should be able to move smoothly from side to side, forward and back, with no physical impingements. You should practice these movements until they feel completely free and flexible while maintaining the energized, aligned body position.

Earlier I mentioned that the difficulty experienced in approaching certain tasks is often due to issues of habit that singers bring. For instance, some singers may habitually lean the upper torso backward, creating excessive sway in the back. When the lower abdominal muscles pull the pelvis forward, thereby bringing the upper back to a more aligned position, it feels to the singer as if the body is leaning awkwardly forward. In reality, it is simply in alignment. Other singers habitually allow the head to lean forward in varying degrees. This is common. For them, to hold the head in an erect position feels strangely affected. What has become a normal habit for the singer creates a limiting dysfunction. Many of these problems can be solved with the exercises discussed here, but establishing new norms always requires mindful repetition.

I have often heard from singers that they have been told to tuck in the abdomen either before or after they inhale. I assume that this is an effort to somehow brace the body to "support" the voice. (I talk about "support" in the next chapter, a term I don't particularly relish.) I believe that the engagement of the core to pull the pelvis forward as described here is the equivalent of that abdominal tuck. The main difference is that I see it as a function of posture, not one of inhalation. Proper body alignment requires the lower abdominals to pull the pelvis forward, which provides the firm grounding needed for good breath management. During inhalation, the upper abdomen must remain relaxed enough to allow the lowering of the diaphragm to initiate inhalation. An abdominal tuck that is not associated with body alignment might cause extraneous tensions that can inhibit the diaphragm's descent. Proper postural alignment can leave the upper abdomen free to make room for a deep breath and can provide the firm lower grounding needed for good breath management. More on this in the chapter on breathing.

If good posture is not the norm for a singer, I suggest trying to change the norm in everyday circumstances, not just when singing. Forming new habits is not easy. I suggest that the singer try focusing on it for just ten minutes a day, twice a day, while walking, while standing in conversation with someone, or while doing some other daily activity. Then I recommend increasing the length of the focus periods in realistic increments. Gradually, a more active and consistent awareness will develop, and proper alignment will become more natural.

When the body is tall and in alignment, with the head balanced on the spine, the singer is ready to breathe with ease and efficiency! The next chapter, on breath management, builds on that aligned body.

Part II

THE THREE STEPS:
ONE STEP AT A TIME

Step 1: "Open Body" and Breath Management

$\mathcal{H}$aving set up the guidelines for aligning the body, the singer is ready to approach breath management. It is the first step of the process that my former student has nicknamed "OOFing." Keep in mind that maintaining the body's alignment is foundational to all aspects of good singing and requires constant attention until it becomes the new norm, the new natural. It allows the expansion of the body's breathing apparatus needed for good breath management. The first *O* of OOFing, then, represents the physical directive Open Body. It serves as a focal point for developing the kinesthetic experience of respiration for singing—both inhalation and exhalation.

Once the goals of the Open Body are achieved, the groundwork is laid for the Open Throat, the second step of the Three-Step Approach, addressed in the next chapter. The Open Throat is a major contributor to resonance, but it cannot function well unless the body is managing the breath well. Therefore, when singers sometimes address the quality of tone as a first step, it is putting the cart before the horse, so to speak. Before we consider resonance, it is important that we understand the function of breath management and be reasonably secure with it. Similarly, before we work on the third step, Forward Articulation, a kinesthetic understanding of resonance is necessary. Building a vocal technique one step at a time is a hallmark of the Three-Step Approach. It builds a secure foundation for each additional layer of skill development. Ultimately, all three steps are integrated and act as a unit to enable fine tone and to allow the development of refined skills, as addressed in part III. Moving step by step in an orderly layering can facilitate beautiful tones, often surprisingly quickly.

The intentionally simple physical directives of the Three-Step Approach are relatively easy to understand and often easy to execute. However, there is no guarantee of instant consistency. Constant focus on each of the three steps is required until new habits are formed and the steps can be integrated. This is true of any skill development, not just singing. Skill development will be up and down before consistency is achieved, and this is normal in the learning curve.

The quality of practice is crucial. Rather than getting caught up in extraneous distractions, practicing with a mindful focus on the most critical elements of a skill is the most direct path to success. For now, the attention is solely on breath management as an independent kinesthetic experience.

I have found that there is no other single area of singing that is as misunderstood as the process of respiration. Considering that we breathe all day long and every day of our lives, this is a little puzzling. While there certainly might be poor breathers out there, most people probably breathe pretty well with the muscles and structures they were born with. What might the reasons be for confusion about breath management?

The term that has most commonly been used for singers' breathing is "breath support." It is so common that one would think that everyone should know exactly what it means, but this is not the case. When new singers walk into my studio for the first time—beginning, intermediate, or advanced—I always ask them to verbalize their understanding of the process of breathing for singing. They almost always have a terribly difficult time putting it into words, even the more advanced singers. Often they throw in the term "breath support" to show that they know what they're supposed to do, but when I ask them what they mean by that term, they can't explain it. Sometimes they talk about "energy," but when asked to explain what that is, they are hard pressed for words. It is the same with the phrase "engaging the body." What is engaged and where? Not being able to answer these questions is more than disconcerting to advanced singers, but I try to soften the jolt by assuring them that they are not alone in their confusion. (Most beginners are not as bothered with their lack of understanding of the breathing process, because they don't bring as many presuppositions with them.)

Only occasionally have I found a singer—at any level—who could describe respiration for singers in a way that made sense physiologically. I think there are a lot of reasons for this confusion, but one culprit might be terminology. The term "breath support," taken at face value, sounds like lifting or supporting something heavy with your breath, and that sounds like excess to me.

I am reminded here of a direction that was given to me when I was a young singer and that, I hear, has been given to a lot of singers over the course of their studies. I remember being told that at the peak of inhalation, just before singing, I should prepare the body as if I am about to move a piano. Sound familiar? It was intended to "energize" the body and was equated to "breath support." For me—and I think for many others—it resulted in a grunt position of the body, especially in the abdominal area. Although I understand what was being sought by the suggestion, particularly for singers whose bodies are de-energized, I think it mistakenly encourages abdominal rigidity and is therefore not conducive to fine breath management. Such images might be appropriate for a person with low energy, but it still sounds like grunting to me. Grunting is antithetical to flexibility and buoyancy, prerequisites for fine breath management. I like to think of breath management as serving the tone rather than supporting it.

Because the term "breath support" may all too easily encourage misconceptions, it is not used in this book. To take its place, the term "breath management" or "breath control" is used. Both are more analogous to the nature of breathing for singing than the term "breath support." Not all confusion can be cleared up with the change of a single term, but I think that it is a significant change and at least a good start to this discussion.

Singers tell me that they hear varying opinions about breath management, and this understandably adds to their confusion. What is often mysterious and elusive for them could be conceptually much simpler. Unlike resonance, for which varying personal preferences for tone are defensible, breathing is a physiologically well-defined process that should elicit consensus on how the mechanism works. Confusion might stem more from the manner in which breath management has been communicated than from the actual facts being presented.

The Three-Step Kinesthetic Approach focuses only on those physical elements of the breathing process that are absolutely necessary for the singer to understand to facilitate proper functioning. While detailed knowledge of physiology is an indispensable asset for the voice teacher, the application of that information is most important for the singer. Singing is not as much an academic endeavor as a kinesthetic one. With clear terminology and simple directives, this chapter focuses on developing the kinesthetic intelligence needed to facilitate fine breath management. It is the beginning of building technical skill step by step.

An intentionally abbreviated explanation of the breathing process begins the foray into breath management to give context to the exercises that follow. The guided exercises are included in this section. In their simplicity, they are designed to elicit the kinesthetic experience of good breath management. These exercises are primarily for the body. They do not yet focus on the quality of resonance, and only two of them incorporate phonation.

THE CONTEXT:
THE KINESTHETIC EXPERIENCE OF THE OPEN BODY

The process of respiration consists of two stages: inhalation and exhalation. Inhalation requires a fuller breath than everyday breathing because the demands of singing are greater than in speech. Exhalation for singing is even more dissimilar from everyday breathing. The singer must manage the release of air with a control that is not otherwise necessary for everyday breathing. The release of breath must be carefully managed, not just exhaled. Although most of the breathing exercises offered here do not include singing, they do set up the body in ways that are needed for singing. The next chapter, on the Open Throat, more directly integrates singing with breath management.

Inhalation: The Body as Initiator and Receptacle

The diaphragm and ribs are important physical structures involved in the process of inhalation. An understanding of their role in breathing is helpful in the exercises that follow.

The diaphragm is a thin muscular sheet shaped like a double dome, and it spreads across the body from the front to the back, connecting to the sternum (breastbone), ribs, and spine. The part of the body above it—the upper torso, or thorax—houses the lungs and heart. Below it, the lower torso houses the intestines and other organs. The diaphragm cannot be seen by the naked eye, but it works quite naturally with every breath you take. The lowering diaphragm presses on the organs below it a bit, causing the upper abdomen—the front area of the body between the sternum and the waist—to expand. This can be seen. The lowering of the diaphragm and resulting expansion are what give the singer the feeling of taking a deep breath rather than a shallow one. However, the ribs also play an important role in the singer's full breath.

Simultaneous with the diaphragm lowering, the ribs expand. Together, these actions produce a vacuum in the lungs that sucks in air. The lungs are flexible organs attached to the ribs and encased by them. They are receptacles for air but can expand and fill with air only if the expanding rib cage to which they are attached creates more space by pulling them outward.

How do the ribs expand? A set of muscles between the ribs, when contracted, pulls the ribs outward. Because of their angle, these muscles pull slightly upward as well as outward. This is important to remember because if a lift of the rib cage is not present, the outward expansion will be limited. The whole inhalation, including the lowering diaphragm and rib expansion, might be referred to as "down-out-and-up movement of the thorax." For the sake of brevity, the muscles of rib expansion are referred to here as the "out-and-up muscles."

Singers often experience the lowering diaphragm and expanding ribs as being "pushed" down and out. This is understandable, but I think it is a misconception worth mentioning here. The diaphragm lowers, not because it pushes down, but because it contracts. The contraction diminishes the surface area of the diaphragm, minimizing the double-dome outline of the higher, more relaxed position. Similarly, the ribs expand because the muscles between them contract, thereby pulling the ribs in an outward direction. They do not push the ribs outward. Therefore, it is better to think of the efforts of expansion as pulling outward as opposed to pushing outward. Not only is it more correct, but it is more congruent with the lifted and buoyant feeling that is desirable for singing. A feeling of push can lead to a locked position of the body that is associated with grunting. Grunting is antithetical to singing!

In everyday breathing, the diaphragm and rib muscles facilitate inhalation, and their relaxation accounts for exhalation. Breathing for singing requires these same muscles, but the manner with which they are used is different, especially in the exhalation process. Strange as it may seem, the control of exhalation for singing is managed largely by the same muscles that facilitate inhalation. More on that in the next section, on exhalation.

Finally, since the rib cage encases the upper torso, the expansion must include the entire circumference of the upper body, back, front, and sides. The sensation of being expanded in this way has often been likened to a barrel of air, a large tire, or a balloon. The singer's need for more air to sing long musical phrases requires maximizing the breath intake.

The physicality of inhalation as described here is abbreviated by the term "Open Body," the first step of the Three-Step Approach. This short verbal prompt should assist in recalling and creating the air-filled buoyancy of an expanded thorax. It also helps with maintaining those efforts while singing.

EXERCISE—INHALATION

The singer should practice the following exercise slowly and mindfully with the focus being on good postural alignment and the Open Body. In preparation for the inhalation, drop the jaw loosely, as if beginning a yawn. (A full yawn creates undesirable tensions.) Such a loose opening allows the breath freer access to the body, especially handy when quick catch breaths are required. The yawning breath is also important in opening the resonating cavities, discussed in the next chapter. As you do the following exercise, make mental note of the physical sensations that accompany the inhalation.

- Stand tall with a singer's posture—the body in alignment.
- Loosely drop the jaw, as if beginning a yawn, so that your inhalation will flow smoothly through the open mouth and throat.
- Take a breath, beginning with a slight bulge of the upper abdomen, the outward manifestation of the diaphragm lowering. If you are not sure whether this is happening, take a moment and lie on the floor. Place your hand on your upper abdomen, the area between the sternum and waist. As you breathe, feel the rise and fall of the abdomen. This is a natural way of breathing and one that you will want to incorporate when you are upright and preparing to sing.
- Almost simultaneous to the abdominal bulge, focus on the ribs. They should be lifting and expanding. Such rib expansion can be felt by placing both hands on the lower ribs at the sides as you breathe.

Trap: Be careful that you don't raise the shoulders or chest while breathing. Once a singer has good alignment with good posture, there is no need to raise either the shoulders or the chest any higher. Doing so produces unnecessary tension and inhibits the inhalation process. Use a mirror to help you monitor this.

Trap: In an effort to feel the abdominal bulge, be careful not to try to force or push the abdominal area out. The abdominal area should bulge slightly as a result of the diaphragm lowering, not as a muscular function independent of breathing. Trying to push the abdomen out is a misplaced effort and has nothing to do with breathing. Rather than the buoyant lifted feeling of air-filled spaces, a heavy, static position is set up that gives the feeling of having eaten too much! Singers are rightly told to breathe low via the lowering diaphragm and the bulging abdomen, but they can often interpret that to mean that the breath is complete if their abdomen sticks out. In fact, because the low breath is so often mentioned, singers sometimes function as if the lungs are behind the abdomen! The lungs, housed within the rib cages, are the receptacles of air, not the abdomen. Therefore, if the expansion does not include rib expansion, a full breath is not possible.

- Fill the lungs, the receptacles of the air, feeling the depth of the descending diaphragm and the width of the expanding rib cage. Since the ribs encase the thorax, the entire circumference of the thorax expands.

Although greater breath intake is needed for singing than for everyday speaking, one does not have to expand to the point of being uncomfortable. Advanced singers who may have been overworking their breathing system may have to relax the effort a bit and seek more flexibility in the abdominal area. Yet, beginners may have to overdo this in the beginning just to find new space in the body.

As I mention in the introduction, even the simplest directions can sometimes be misconstrued, causing the singer to fall into certain traps. These traps can be daunting to be sure. One can see how they might contribute to the confusion about breath management. However, if the singer stays focused on the relatively simple physical directions being given rather than what habit dictates or what seems most familiar, the traps can be avoided. As always, the focus must be primarily on the aligned and actively opened body.

With greater awareness of the possible traps, repeat the exercise several times, trying not to succumb to any of them. Mindful repetition gives new insight, which in turn leads to new habits. Look for a feeling of lift and buoyancy in the body. Use only the energy necessary to achieve this with no extraneous tensions coming into play.

The feeling of being buoyant is important and is related to maintained expansion, a crucial element of the exhalation process. It is the opposite of squeezing, pushing, or grunting—all inhibitory actions created by inward and downward rib muscles, as opposed to the outward and upward muscles that are responsible for good rib expansion. Squeezing the body, collapsing, or pushing the breath out should be avoided at all costs. Instead, the body should maintain its expansion in a state of suspension. The difference between muscles used as agents of opening the body for expansion and those used as agents of closing the body is a critical distinction in many areas of singing technique. It is the difference between good tensions and bad tensions, good singing and bad singing. Focusing on the lift and expansion of the body is the goal of the first of the Three Steps: Open Body.

Breathing as a singer may not feel "natural" at first, but it becomes that way. The feeling of suspended buoyancy is a balance between properly contracted muscles that expand the body and the natural tendency of those muscles to relax. Although taking full breaths requires muscular effort, that effort should never lose its flexibility or freedom of movement. No unnecessary tension should be allowed to creep into the breathing process. Every movement or task can be done with more or less tension, but doing it with only the work needed and not any more is the best path to follow.

Singing longer phrases on one breath is not the only reward of good breath management. The very tone itself will be positively affected in terms of its clarity, volume, beauty, and flexibility. With good breath management, there is no danger of either spilling too much air or strangling off the air.

Exhalation: Controlled Release of Air

With the expansive buoyancy of a full breath, the singer is on the way to beautifully free singing. However, it is at the juncture between inhalation and singing that the rubber hits the road. This is the point at which the singer's inhalation must morph into a controlled release of air in a manner that best serves the needs of a good singing tone.

Consciously or not, young singers often provide air to the tone in one of two ways: by simply collapsing the expansion or by pulling in the abdominal muscles in an effort to push the air out. Allowing a body to collapse expels air in an excessive and uncontrollable manner. Forcing air out of the body is excessive and runs the risk of creating extraneous tensions that will inhibit the mechanisms of breath and resonance. Neither technique manages the breath as needed for fine singing. Advanced singers who do not have a secure understanding of breath management are more creative in how they control the breath, some more egregious than others!

The controlled release of air for singing requires much the same muscular efforts as those of inhalation. That doesn't mean that the singer is inhaling the tone but that the muscles of inhalation are important in judiciously regulating the air flow for both initiating and sustaining efficient singing tones. To sustain long musical phrases, the diaphragm and rib muscles must maintain the actively contracted muscles longer than for everyday breathing. This is work.

Being that the contracted muscles of the ribs and diaphragm are not used to the same degree in daily breathing, they tend to be underdeveloped. Therefore, to be utilized in new ways, they must not only be managed but strengthened for endurance. From my earlier teaching days, I remember working with a big, brawny jock, clearly in great physical shape. However, after fifteen minutes of working on maintaining rib expansion, he complained bitterly about the aching in his ribs and back. The rib muscles had not been part of his daily workouts or crucial to the sports that he was involved in. They *are* crucial to singing.

The following exercises are designed to sharpen the singers' awareness of the balance needed between the efforts of maintained body expansion and the regulated flow of breath.

EXERCISE—BALANCING THE EFFORTS

- Take a yawning breath while focusing on the Open Body as described in the exercise for inhalation. After the body is comfortably full, maintain the expansion in the body for several seconds while making mental note of what you are doing to accomplish this. Use these moments to raise your consciousness of the balance in your body. Maintain the efforts of inhalation—the downward thrust of the diaphragm and outward pull on the ribs—with no new muscular effort introduced. You will be holding your breath with an expanded body in a suspended, buoyant state.

- While maintaining the expanded and buoyant thorax known here as the Open Body, focus on what you are doing (or not doing) to maintain this position. Repeat the process several times, each time paying attention to the sensations in the body when maintaining expansion after inhalation. These sensations, along with others to be discussed, should continue during singing. They contribute to the kinesthetic experience of good breath management.

The peak of expansion is the ideal position of the body for the onset of tone. At this point, it is neither collapsing nor pushing, neither inhaling nor exhaling. This poised position reminds me of the moment in time when a ball tossed up in the air reaches the peak of the ascent before starting its descent. You will be at the peak of your breath without introducing any new direction, any turnaround. Although we know that the diaphragm and rib muscles are contracted to accomplish the expansion, there is no new tension or effort needed to begin singing. One often sees a singer "set" the body just before singing. This is not necessary and may lock the system. Just concentrate for now on maintaining the feeling of depth, lift, and width that produced the complete breath.

It is this feeling of the expanded Open Body remaining in suspension that is integral to good breath management for singing. It is the optimum condition for providing the singing tone with just the right amount of air to sing beautifully and flexibly. It relates to the *appoggio*, an Italian term that refers to the body's role in managing the breath. One sings with this expanded and suspended Open Body and, in doing so, manages the breath without creating any constrictions in the throat.

Trap: One of the ways that you might be tempted to hold the breath is to firmly set the body as in an isometric crunch of the abdominal muscles, virtually a grunt position. While this does indeed hold the air back, it limits the body's flexibility and causes constriction in the throat. It more or less locks the body in a static state. Sometimes singers are so concerned with adding "energy" to the system that they overdo the focus on rock-hard abs, as if preparing to resist a fist against the abdomen. Breath management is flexible, not static.

Trap: Another common mistake in the effort to retain the air involves squeezing any part of your throat—conscious or unconscious—to cork off the air. Most often it goes hand in hand with the abdominal crunch. The release of the air will be hampered, as will a free-flowing tone! To be sure that this is not taking place, the singer should take a little extra breath at the end of the inhalation. There should be no clicking sound in the throat, indicating that it had been closed in some way and needing to be popped open to allow the intake. It should be open during inhalation and during maintained expansion.

In both these traps misplaced efforts to control the breath constrict the breathing mechanism and the resonance system. Those muscular efforts close spaces rather than open them. Open spaces in the breathing apparatus, through maintained expansion, allow open spaces in the resonators. Constricted spaces in the breathing apparatus cause constricted resonators. To demonstrate this, quite apart from your singer's breath, consciously squeeze your abs. Note how the throat reflexively squeezes as well.

The discussion of resonance in the next chapter makes clear that a richly resonated tone is possible only with open and accepting resonators, with the throat being a major resonator. The Open Body serves to enable the open throat.

EXERCISE—CONTROL WITH FLEXIBILITY

The following exercise is designed to avoid both traps just mentioned and to set up proper conditions for managing the air flow.

- With a loosely dropped jaw, initiate a yawning breath with the Open Body, including the lowered diaphragm and expanded rib cage. Maintain the expansion for a few seconds without adding any new muscle action. Take in a tiny bit more, being sure that the throat has remained open and that there is no clicking sound. Note a bit more bulge in the abdomen with the additional intake.
- Now release only that little bit of air just added by a slight pulling in the abdomen, without letting the ribs relax at all. This requires isolating the movement of the abdomen from the maintained expansion of the ribs, lending independence of action to each element. The ongoing outward pull of the rib muscles continues while allowing flexibility of the abdomen for a measured release.
- Repeat this process, adding several new intakes of air and releases while the body remains expanded. Because the repeated intakes of air replenish your breath supply, the body can remain expanded and in suspension for a longer period than without them. The exercise then does not require any diminishment of the rib expansion. Exchanging only a small portion of the total volume of air in the body, slowly breathe in, out, in, out, in, out—as in slow panting. The coordination between the maintenance of expansion and the slight abdominal assist for releasing judicious amounts of air is a good starting point for managing the breath.

The singer needs to maintain the expansion to prevent either collapsing or locking the breath. The first situation creates a weak breathy tone, and the second creates a strangled strident tone. For singing, air must be gently released for a subtle tone or more vigorously provided for a hearty tone or percussive effect. In all situations, the expansive efforts of inhalation must persist, or the breath is not being managed well.

It is natural for contracting muscles to tire, as this is a new use of them and quite different from breathing for everyday speaking. However, singers must keep them working as comfortably as possible. It may take time to develop strength, but use only the necessary amount of strength, power, or effort to accomplish a particular goal and no more.

You may be wondering how the ribs can remain expanded if you're singing a long phrase that requires most of the air you have inhaled. Slowly, the ribs may need to release that air but never with a complete relaxation of the out-and-up muscles. Those muscles continue their active contraction but with flexibility that allows them to regulate the release as needed.

Since the natural tendency is for the muscles to relax, thereby expelling the air uncontrollably, the bulk of one's energy and focus usually has to be toward maintaining the expansion in the body. However, when the tone needs greater breath pressure, such as that for louder or percussive singing, the abdominal muscles play a greater role, as they pull in and upward, judiciously resisted by the lowered diaphragm. This is often described as muscular antagonism because there are two opposing muscle forces. The risk with using that term is that it might invite an unhealthy degree of locking tension in the system that could result in pushing and tightness in the tone. Yet, with too little antagonism between the abdominals and the diaphragm, core strength in the tone would be lacking.

An example of the role of antagonism with flexibility might be that of an archer who draws the arrow back with the pull of his arm muscles, thereby increasing the tautness of the bow. The sudden release of the arrow would be similar to a collapse in the singer's body after an expansive inhalation. If instead of shooting the arrow, the archer decides to gradually release the arrow from the full draw, he would need to maintain the engagement of his arm muscles but lessen that pull little by little to smoothly and slowly allow the arrow to return to its starting position. The antagonism that exists in this situation is between the rebounding tendency of the taut bow and the resisting pull of arm muscles, which manages the release of the bow.

The antagonism between the abdominal muscles and the diaphragm must not become an impasse, as in an isometric crunch. The resistance needed to regulate the breath flow must reflect flexible cooperation between the abdominals and the diaphragm in managing a smooth and even breath flow. This is a balancing act. The slow panting exercise described here should help with this aspect of breath management.

EXERCISE—SUSTAINING THE RELEASE

Keeping in mind both the maintained expansion and the abdomen's role in providing air flow, try the following exercises.

- With a loosely dropped jaw, take a yawning breath. Maintain it for a few seconds without adding any additional or unnecessary tensions to hold back the air. Now exhale on a soft "sh" sound for as long as you can sustain it. The first area of the body to move inward toward expulsion of the air should be in the abdominal area but only gently since the "sh" should be soft and sustained for a long time. After that, the ribs may join in even as the outward efforts of the rib muscles continue. The chest should remain erect as a function of good posture. Try this several times, noting the functions of the abdomen, the diaphragm, and the ribs as you try to extend the "sh" sound for longer and longer periods.

Trap: The "sh" sound is created by the tongue's lifted position in the mouth. The sides of the tongue touch the front upper part of the mouth, called the "hard palate," leaving some space in the middle, through which the air passes. This requires only a small degree of air restriction, more like a redirection of air, so be sure that the restriction is not more than needed. You must rely on the body to control the air flow, not undue restriction from the "sh" sound. (I prefer the "sh" to the commonly used hard "s" because is entails less restriction of the air.)

EXERCISE—ISOLATING THE DIAPHRAGM AND RIB MUSCLES WITH REPEATED UTTERANCES

- After the gentle expulsion of air in the aforementioned exercise, try speaking a soft "ha" with a dropped jaw three times on three short notes but not percussively. Take small breaths after each utterance. Repeat this after a fuller breath. This should feel similar to the slow panting exercise in that the abdomen will be governing the stopping and starting of tone, but the chest or ribs should not become involved in the pulsing.
- Change the volume level several times, and note the changes in the body, especially in the abdominals. The abdominals should pull in as vigorously as your volume increases, but the chest and rib cage should stay stable. This requires independence of both the diaphragm–abdomen partnership and the continuing rib expansion.

Trap: It is common when doing this exercise that the chest and rib pulse along with each abdominal pulse. This means that independence of action has been compromised, that the Open Body is not being maintained, and that breath management is breaking down. Because of this, the quality of a tone produced would be negatively affected. Remember that short repeated tones must be built on a stable body the same as longer sustained tones.

If a singer has become caught up in excessive tensions—possibly in an exaggerated effort to "support" his or her voice, limit breath flow, or push—special attention must be given to creating freer flow and more flexibility. Sometimes these tensions are a result of trying to create a tone, particularly a big, operatic tone, without proper breath management to serve the cause. The singer knows well that a breathy tone is not desirable, and he or she may figure out, consciously or unconsciously, that squeezing the body can prevent breathiness. It is an unfortunate shortcut that causes a tight, strident tone. This is not the answer to breathiness.

In such a case, a singer will have to work on letting go of the constrictive hold, particularly in the abdominals or throat, even if the tone temporarily becomes a little breathy. This requires some patience and might feel like a regression to the singer. Constrictions are like crutches. To throw them away gives a feeling of helplessness. The singer might experience letting go as breathiness or loss of power even when this is not so. When the tone is not strapped with tension, the power is being released from the body rather than held by it. As soon as the singer learns to maintain the Open Body, it will not be necessary to use dysfunctional crutches to hold back the air. Singers will then experience a freer tone!

More often than not, the beginning singer has not developed the tensions described here. Usually, the beginner tends to err toward having little or no outward muscle pull to maintain the expansion and manage the breath, with the result being the weak, breathy tone. However, collapse can also cause some tensions, as the singer may feel the need to compensate for breathiness. Instruction in creating and maintaining the Open Body should eradicate those tendencies rather quickly if the bad habits are not too ingrained.

In anticipation of the next chapter, on the Open Throat and its role in resonance, pitch is added to the earlier exercise, as shown in figure 3.1. This vocalization once again requires individual portions of air flow for each syllable with a small breath between each one. However, the stability of the Open Body must not be disturbed. The activity is solely at the level of the abdomen and is subtle unless singing at loud volumes.

As with most pitched vocalizations in this book, the treble clef will be used for the sake of expediency. In all vocalizations, the pitches given in the figures are only suggestions. The singer should always choose a comfortable pitch in the middle range.

The symbol shown for "ha" in figure 3.1 is extracted from the International Phonetic Alphabet—in this case, similar to the letters of the English alphabet. A selected list of IPA symbols is found in the appendix and is discussed more thoroughly in subsequent chapters.

Figure 3.1.   Abdominal activity and vocalization.

- Stand tall and balanced as described in chapter 2, on posture.
- Loosely drop the jaw, preparing for the open vowel sound in "ha."
- Initiate the inhalation with the lowering diaphragm and expanding rib cage. Note the expansion around the circumference of the thorax.
- Be careful not to raise the shoulders or chest while breathing.
- Use a slightly aspirated [h] in the exercise, but don't exaggerate that element.
- When beginning the first tone, be judicious in the amount of inward abdominal pull you use. It takes very little. Concentrate mainly on the stability of the expanded Open Body.
- Because you are partially replenishing the breath after each of the three short notes, you should not notice any decrease in the rib expansion, only slight pulses in the abdominal area.
- At the end of the first measure, release the contractions of diaphragm and rib muscles, but don't let your chest fall. The erect chest is a constant element, one of correct body alignment.
- When you take the breath after the momentary relaxation, focus on the down-out-and-up expansion of the thorax, independent of a stable, erect chest.
- Try this vocalization at varying levels of volume, and notice the demand on the body. Be sure to maintain the lift of the body at all volume levels even if the abdominal muscles become more energized.

SUMMARY

The Open Body is represented by the first *O* in OOFing and is the focal point of good breath management. It refers to a well-lowered diaphragm and expanded rib cage with voluminous air in the lungs. It refers to continuing efforts of the muscles of inhalation, even as air is provided as needed. The release of that air is judiciously managed by the same muscular efforts that created the intake of the air, along with the balanced antagonism between the lowered diaphragm and inward pull of the abdominals. This process is diametrically opposed to squeezing the body, pushing, blowing, or collapsing.

Before we move on to the chapter on resonance, I should note that breathing for singing is not only a matter of opening the body; inhalation also plays an important role in preparing the Open Throat required of full resonance. Breathing with a dropped, yawning jaw as suggested in the exercises is just one part of that preparation.

The Open Body is a requirement of the Open Throat, the second *O* in the OOFing mantra and the subject of the next chapter. Working together, they enable full resonance and allow the tone to exit freely through air-filled spaces. Issues of resonance are presented only as integrated with issues of breath management, because their integration is necessary for achieving the kinesthetic experience that enables a well-resonated tone.

• 4 •

Step 2: "Open Throat" and Resonance

The second O of the OOFing mantra refers to the Open Throat. The throat, more formally called the *pharynx*, is an important resonator of vocal sound, as are the mouth and nose. Together, they combine to form a single, complex, and malleable resonance system. These cavities have the potential of enriching the sound, coloring it, and giving it size. The Open Throat prompt relates to all three resonators but focuses most on the pharynx.

Compared to breath management, resonance might seem more complex and elusive. Because breathing is an everyday occurrence, the mechanics of breath management might be easier to grasp once a clear explanation is offered; one can *see* the physicality of erect posture, slightly bulging abdominals, and expanded thorax. While singers understand well the relationship between these physical signs and the ability to sing long phrases, they might not understand the direct relationship between breath management and resonance. While most indications of resonance are invisible, primarily *heard*, they are enabled by the Open Body and Open Throat, both of which are kinesthetic experiences with specific physical attributes.

A singer's personal experience of resonance is subjective and limited. If a singer has never experienced the full potential of his or her resonating system, full and free resonance is completely uncharted territory. The discovery process might well entail some trepidation. The singer doesn't know where the process is headed, has never been there before, and has to proceed with trust until the new sounds are experienced. It can be frightening or exciting or both.

Before we begin exercises for creating the Open Throat, I offer a brief overview of the nature of resonance to put the exercises in the appropriate context. Phonation, the sound created by vibrating vocal folds, is also discussed.

Facilitating the Open Throat is a critical juncture in the process of learning how to sing beautifully. As the exercises are introduced, it will become apparent that the layering process described in the overview of the Three Steps must be integrative. The potential for a fully resonating tone will be enabled only as the Open Body integrates with the Open Throat, allowing the natural laws of resonance to function optimally.

In the next chapter, when Forward Articulation is introduced as the third step, all Three Steps will merge to function as one unit. Together, they provide the grounding of a vocal technique that is equipped for highly specialized functioning.

THE CONTEXT

Resonance enhances the initial sound created by the vibrations of the vocal folds, which function primarily in a reflexive mode in reaction to the stimulus of air flow. Although the internal workings of the vocal folds and related structures are physiologically complex, phonation functions well if given the proper physical conditions. The Three Steps encourage these conditions.

Phonation

Phonation is quite natural, beginning with the baby's first cry. Since phonation is largely reflexive, trying to directly "operate" the vocal folds is a bit like trying to "operate" your eyes or ears. The vocal folds work if they are healthy and have the right stimulus: proper air flow.

The vocal folds (sometimes inaccurately referred to as *vocal cords*) are flexible muscular structures located in the larynx (sometimes called the *voice box*), at the lower end of the pharynx. Air passing through the folds causes them to vibrate, creating vocal sound known as *phonation*. The vocal folds can produce tones throughout a large pitch range by changing their size, shape, and tension. With the help of good breath management and good resonance, they can also assist in creating loud tones and soft ones and everything between.

The so-called Adam's apple can often be seen as a bulge in the front of the neck. This notch is at the top of one of the laryngeal cartilages. The folds are attached to the inner side of this cartilage at a point slightly below the notch, and this is the level at which phonation occurs.

Although *phonation* refers specifically to vocal production, the sound produced by wind instruments functions much like the sound created by the voice. In the oboe, for instance, air passing through the reeds sets them into vibration, thereby creating sound. In both cases, the vibrations created are a response to the air flow. Air flow can be consciously and physically controlled.

In the eighteenth and early-nineteenth centuries, a manner of singing referred to as the *bel canto* style suggested a technique for fine or beautiful singing. It was particularly prescriptive about breathing for singers. Although there are differences of opinion regarding when that style was so named or how it was used, it is considered to be a technique that extols free-flowing tone sufficient in size to fill large halls and carry over an orchestra. An old adage related to traditional vocal techniques such as the *bel canto* technique suggests that any singer who knows how to breathe knows how to sing. With regard to phonation, it might be said that any singer who knows how to breathe and resonate knows how to phonate!

This assumes that the structures for phonation are healthy. While functional problems in the singing technique can be averted and often solved by employing healthy techniques, such as those suggested in the Three-Step Approach, medical problems require the supervision of a physician. Physicians often collaborate with voice teachers and voice therapists as part of a prescriptive plan for restoring vocal health.

Resonance

Phonation is only the beginning. As with the oboe, the sound waves produced are unremarkable and unusable without the help of resonators. To produce an audibly good tone, the sound must go through one or more resonators. In the case of the oboe, that resonator is the body of the oboe. In the case of the singer, the resonators are the throat, mouth, and nose. It is commonly acknowledged that the larynx, the lower section of the throat, is a resonator that contributes ring to the voice.

Since resonance production is largely an internal phenomenon—a process that is mostly invisible to the naked eye—it can be a perplexing mystery to the singer. However, with a basic understanding of how resonators function in relation to the rest of their bodies, the singer will be much more likely to utilize them effectively.

For most people, creating beautiful resonance is not a priority in everyday circumstances. Unlike singers, nonsingers might find that their "natural" untrained voice serves their needs adequately even though it is not particularly resonant or beautiful. However, people who use their speaking voice professionally often need to work on improving their vocal production much like singers. Without adequate resonance, volume, or clarity of articulation, they might appear to lack professional presence and authority, or their voice might tire easily. These voice users will need to correct problems such as lack of volume, hoarseness, excessive nasality, or inappropriate pitch level. Depending on the specific problem, consultation with a qualified physician, speech therapist, or voice teacher would be well advised.

Serious singers need a well-developed vocal technique to sing demanding arias and art songs with ease and beauty. A good technique is also the vehicle for musical creativity and expressivity. This goes far beyond the "natural" abilities of an untrained singer. The Three-Step Approach offers a perspective and systematic process to build an effective technique and refine it.

The resonating system, as complex as it is, can be most simply described as a system of air-filled cavities. Any cavity—be it a bottle, tube, or pharynx—possesses pitch properties. Blowing across the top of an empty sixteen-ounce soda bottle produces a sound with a particular pitch. That pitch is said to be the frequency of the bottle. Blowing across an empty thirty-two-ounce bottle produces a particular pitch as well, but it will be lower than what the sixteen-ounce bottle produces. Pitches are resonated best by cavities whose size and shape result in frequencies that are most in tune with the frequencies created by the vocal folds. By sympathetically vibrating with them, the air-filled cavities enhance the emitted tone greatly. This contributes beauty, color, and size to the voice, largely by-products of the laws of resonance.

In this way, resonance is enabled rather than made, and it is maximized by skilled singers. Not all resonators are the same. Singers must discover the potential size, shape, and flexibility of their cavities to unearth the potential resonance therein. Just as two similar but different soda bottles produce different pitches, two singers' resonance systems give individual and unique results, but the underlying principles of function remain the same.

Fortunately, the pharynx and mouth are flexible cavities that can be adjusted by the singer. (The nose is not as changeable, but the degree to which it is used can be easily regulated.) Through adjustments, cavities can become sympathetic resonators to a wide variety of pitches and vowels. Without a receptive cavity, putting a tone through it would be like putting a square peg in a round hole. Inadequacy of the breath system is often the reason for inadequate flexibility in the throat and most likely the cause of flatting.

Although resonance adjustments might seem daunting, once the singer achieves a good balance between the conscious opening of the throat and its flexibility, many of the adjustments happen quite easily. With flexible and receptive cavities, the laws of resonance take over, allowing the singer to produce richly enhanced tone with the least possible effort. It is a real bargain and a perk every singer should take advantage of.

The pharynx, a major resonating cavity, contributes richness to the voice. It is comfortably but intentionally opened for singing. This is the motivation behind the Open Throat prompt of the OOFing mantra. Once the singer understands the underlying principles behind it, this simple directive gives focus to the correct thought process and, with it, the correct physical action.

While much resonance is produced in areas that cannot be seen, it can be greatly affected by structures that can be seen. The back wall of the throat, the mouth itself, and the jaw are all structures that can be easily seen and adjusted for purposes of better resonance. The tongue can also influence resonance, and these movements are more thoroughly discussed in chapter 5, on Forward Articulation. That chapter makes clear that articulation itself is a form of resonance adjustment. For every vowel and consonant, there is a separate and unique resonance adjustment. More on that later.

As discussed, the lower part of the pharynx is called the *larynx*, the housing of the vocal folds. The middle pharynx is called the *oropharynx* because it is the area of the pharynx behind the oral cavity, the mouth. It partially be seen by opening the mouth and looking in a mirror. The upper part of the pharynx, known as the *nasopharynx*, leads to the nasal cavity, the nose. Each of the three sections of the pharynx, surrounded and connected with a variety of soft tissue and muscle, has a specific role to play in the adjustment of resonance.

The variety of muscles can be a blessing or a curse for the singer. After all, the mouth and pharynx process our food intake by chewing and swallowing it. If those same muscles are activated while trying to sing, the singer is in big trouble. As you are reading this, try imitating the swallowing action. I think you will see that it is antithetical to singing! Utilizing the swallowing muscles is to be avoided at all costs when singing, but doing so is more common than one would think. Singers must learn to use the flexibility of the resonating system in ways that are the opposite of those used in the process of eating. Rather than squeezing to push the food down, muscles need to open spaces to create air-filled resonating cavities.

If the Open Throat is integrated with the Open Body, the two can elicit beauty, richness, and ring in the vocal sound quite quickly. As with all other kinds of skill development, however, constant reminders are needed to build new habits, and consistency will take time. Reminders can come from one's internal voice if the concepts are understood well or from the external voice of a teacher. In either case, it is important to keep the eye on the ball, so to speak. The simplicity of the three OOFing prompts helps greatly as reminders and guideposts for recalling the correct kinesthetic experiences.

There may be some concern about any direct attention given to the throat for the purposes of creating resonance. I understand the concern because all too often we hear singers, even advanced ones, insert some of the swallowing muscles into their vocal production. This gives rise to a muffled, swallowed, or otherwise inhibited sound that is clearly objectionable. There could be many reasons for this dysfunctional use of the voice, including improper breathing, poor tonal concept, or misconceptions about resonance production. However, it must be made clear that the Open Throat is not the cause of a "throaty" tone. It is quite the opposite. A "throaty" tone is one in which some muscle or muscles are impinging on the space in the throat, thereby closing the throat to greater or lesser degree. This is often caused by inappropriate activation of the swallowing muscles. Consequently, the listener is uncomfortably aware of throat interference. Properly resonated tone should be heard only as tone, not tone and muscle. Encouraging the Open Throat as a flexible air-filled cavity provides freedom of air flow and resonance, the antithesis of a "throaty" tone.

Many singers and teachers rightfully fear what is sometimes referred to as "manipulation" of the throat. It is a pejorative use of the word that indicates a faulty technique with problems of tension where it doesn't belong. However, to label all muscular activity as "manipulative" in this sense is to blur the distinction between good tensions and bad tensions, the right muscles and the wrong muscles. I think it is a problem of semantics, not unlike those involved in labeling a tone as "throaty." I prefer the definition of "manipulate" as found in the *New Oxford Dictionary* (2005): "Handle and control, typically in a skillful manner." This is quite a different way of looking at manipulation and, by extension, might be applied to creating the Open Throat. Skillfully engaging muscles that have the capability to open the throat contributes positively to creating an open and receptive resonating cavity. Other muscles that close the throat, like swallowing muscles, must be deactivated because of their adverse effect on the voice.

The overarching principle of vocal resonance is that tone is resonated in air, not muscle. It is of air and in air. Consequently, encouraging the throat to open and become a spacious, air-filled cavity rather than a lax or constricted cavity is the only way to fully unleash a singer's potential for rich resonance. This must be well served by the Open Body.

The Workload

With regard to a singer's muscular work or effort, a general rule to follow is this: Employ only the muscular work needed to achieve a particular result. This is true for both the Open Body and the Open Throat, including the specialized use of large and small muscles associated with them. Learning the difference between good muscle work and bad muscle work is important in a singer's development.

Sometimes, to demonstrate how a physical action can be done with more effort than is necessary, I hold out my forearm in a position parallel to the floor and then bend it upward toward a vertical position near my shoulder. Very simple. Very easy. My hand has moved to shoulder height without any noticeable tension—and this is apparent—even though some muscles are necessarily tensing to accomplish that arm movement. Then I put my forearm back down to the position parallel to the floor, and before bending my arm this time, I tighten the muscles in the arm. In this state of isometric tension, muscles working against muscles, I raise the forearm again to shoulder height with great struggle. Very difficult. Very tiring. And very apparent. The singer cannot afford any such isometric "crunches" in the body, as they severely limit flexibility and venture into deadlock.

The Alexander technique, a well-known system of body awareness and functionality, is mentioned in chapter 2, on posture, because of its focus on proper alignment. It seeks to free the body of unnecessary, inhibiting tensions by utilizing and developing those muscles that properly support the body so that its parts are freed for singing, playing the violin, golfing, dancing, or any other physical activity. It requires an energized state of readiness with the body actively resisting the pull of gravity and deactivating extraneous tensions. Body movements performed in this manner can be accomplished with ease and efficiency even as they require the work of muscles.

An energized state of readiness is not accomplished in a state of rest. A resting body cannot jump 2.45 meters in a high jump or run a mile in less than four minutes. Like fine singing, these are uber-natural feats. In breathing for singing, a fine muscular balance must be struck between the effort to maintain expansion of the breathing mechanism while singing and the need to provide air flow for the tone. The Open Body prompt is not just relevant to the role of the Open Throat; it is crucial to it.

The Open Throat is facilitated by muscles that pull the walls of the throat open allowing air to occupy the increased space. The expansion is greater than that of a pharynx at rest or even as used in everyday speech. In contrast to a lax pharynx, the singer's pharynx is an intentionally opened, air-filled cavity, ready to resonate.

Since sound is resonated in air-filled cavities, air is definitely the singer's friend. I know this sounds strange, but many singers have to be reminded of that, particularly some advanced singers who rightfully dread having a breathy tone. Their concern is understandable, but they come to regard the exhaled breath as somewhat of an enemy. Unfortunately, some singers have discovered that if they add a little control in the throat (aka pejorative manipulation), excess air in the tone can be minimized. While this might accomplish that, the constriction in the throat causes the tone to become tight with an unpleasant quality. Those singers have lost sight of the nature of sound itself, namely, air molecules, which have been set in motion by vibrations. Those molecules must be allowed to dance freely in open spaces! This can happen only if the muscles that open those spaces remain active.

Inhibiting the air in the throat in an effort to control the breath is what I sometimes facetiously call "throat support," a version of "breath support." This can be seen in mild cases and in extreme cases and is not uncommon. Of course, breath control should come from the body's management of the breath, not from restricting air in the throat. However, an Open Throat is indeed vulnerable to losing air if it is not managed well in the body. With every step, it becomes clearer that each step is dependent on the other. How this integration enables good resonance is a matter that falls in the realm of kinesthetic experience.

THE KINESTHETIC EXPERIENCE OF THE OPEN THROAT

A kinesthetic experience involves not only the physicality of a particular activity but discerning awareness and control of it. The following exercises approach resonance as an integrative skill and guide the singer toward the complete kinesthetic experience of good resonance.

The guidelines that accompany the exercises are at least as important as the exercises themselves, which are first and foremost physical exercises. The guidelines methodically remind the singer of the intentionality and integration of the Open Throat and Open Body before and during singing. If followed carefully and mindfully, they lead the singer toward creating a flexibly receptive throat, enabling optimum resonance there with the least effort.

A proper inhalation is the primary vehicle for creating the Open Throat as well as the Open Body. Too often inhalation is associated only with filling the lungs with air, not the throat. At the very least, this is a missed opportunity for resonance. The yawning breath and loosely dropped jaw are natural ways to encourage the Open Throat as an air-filled cavity. (Remember that such a yawning breath does not reach the position of a full yawn but only the beginning of it or even the anticipation of it.)

The yawning breath is often suggested in voice studios because it encourages a comfortably dropped larynx, contributing greatly to freedom in the vocal tract. The low larynx has been proven to impart richness as well as ring to the tone. It is not the usual position for everyday speaking but an essential element of fine resonance. As part of the complete inhalation described in chapter 3, the drop of the jaw and lowered larynx should be encouraged, not forced.

Addressing the Open Throat is much like addressing the Open Body in that there are two basic parts of the process: the first is to achieve the desired expansion in preparation for singing; the second is to maintain the expansion during singing. This is explained more fully as the chapter progresses.

To ensure that the Open Throat is accomplished simultaneously with inhalation, the following exercises are divided into five parts: posture, inhalation, consciousness raising, phonating/resonating on spoken tones, and phonating/resonating on sung tones. The first three are preparatory steps for the body and mind, and the last two introduce vocalization.

Posture and inhalation, the first two parts, are discussed in chapters 2 and 3 but are reinforced for the sake of enabling good resonance. The muscular effort used to achieve body alignment and the Open Body is important for resonance. The throat cannot remain open if the body does not maintain its expanded position. This is why it is so important to imprint on the mind and body the sensations experienced at the peak of inhalation before beginning to phonate and resonate. A moment or two of consciousness raising can help with this.

Consciousness raising, the third part, may sound like some New Age meditative practice. Perhaps there are some similarities, but in this context it involves slowing the preparatory process down, which to my mind is a key ingredient of training or retraining the singing voice. At the point of greatest expansion, just before singing, singers often either relax the expansion or lockset it. Mindful pausing at this point can ward off these tendencies, as it allows time for the singer to assimilate the physical sensations of the Open Body/Open Throat. Trying to sing without this preparation would be like building a house on sand. It is worth the time to think it through to get it right, changing habits if necessary.

It would be understandable that singers might want to rush through the first three parts; they want to get on to the parts that include singing! However, the integration sought in those last two parts is only as successful as the preparations in the first three parts. There is much to be learned by moving through the five parts of the kinesthetic experience slowly and methodically, layering a new part on only after the previous one has been properly assimilated. Try not to be impatient. In time and with mindful practice, muscle memory assumes a greater role, and new habits become easier.

Part 1: Posture Preparation

- Assume the position of the aligned body with a lift of the upper torso and stretch of the spine as described in chapter 2. The back should not be swayed, and the head should balance as on a central pivotal point, not leaning forward or back, eyes looking straight ahead. It might be good to review the principles of alignment before going on.

Part 2: Inhalation

- Take a slow, yawning breath with a freely dropped jaw, slight bulge in the front abdominal area as the diaphragm lowers, and plentiful expansion of the rib cage. You must use the breath to accomplish two things simultaneously: the Open Body and the Open Throat. Together, they form a single column of air.
- While inhaling, be sure that the ribs are being comfortably pulled outward, allowing the lungs to fill with air. The shoulders and chest should not rise.
- Simultaneous with the lowering diaphragm and expanding ribs, let the inhaled breath fill the mouth and throat as well as the lungs. Think of the breath as one continuous column of air, including the throat as resonating cavity. You shouldn't have to struggle to take a full breath; instead, *allow* the expansion to happen.
- The yawn should encourage the lowering of the larynx, and this is a good thing. You may recall that a slight bulge in the front of the neck is an indicator of the position of the larynx. If you can locate the protruding notch, try putting a finger on it when your body and throat are completely at rest; then begin your yawning breath. While inhaling, you should feel the notch lowering, indicating that the larynx is lowering. This should be experienced as a release in the throat, not as a forced movement. The full inhalation should create the sensation of a long, deep, vertical, and spacious column from the lowered diaphragm, through the thorax, continuing through the open pharynx and mouth.

Part 3: Consciousness Raising

This is a mental exercise. You are making a studied observation of your body at the peak of inhalation. It is an extremely important step; don't rush through it.

- Once you have found a full-bodied inhalation including the Open Throat, spend some time in this position so that you know how you accomplished it and what it feels like to maintain it.
- Hold the breath just taken for a few seconds by simply maintaining the expanded position at the end of the breath. Don't change anything about the way that the inhalation was taken while holding the breath. Don't relax it. Don't lockset it. Don't close your mouth or your throat. Notice that as long as you maintain your expansion, you will maintain the air. It is quite the opposite of collapsing, squeezing, or pushing the air out. All that is needed to maintain the air is the continuing down-out-and-up muscular efforts. This expansion should not falter when you begin to phonate.
- While maintaining the buoyant expanded position, ask yourself the following questions: Where is the work being done? What does it feel like? Why does the air stay in the body and in the throat? In my experience, most singers who have had a difficult time answering these questions gradually gain awareness of the physicality of this position and the intentionality needed to maintain it. This is an important step in the singer's kinesthetic understanding of breath management and resonance production.

Trap: The tendency for the abdominal area to squeeze and for the throat to close is addressed in one of the traps noted in chapter 3, in the section "Balancing the Efforts." Please refer to that section if you need a reminder. It is important that neither the body nor the throat closes in any manner after inhaling and before singing.

At the peak of inhalation before beginning to sing, air remains accessible, not locked in, and the throat can remain open. The abdominal muscles can amply and freely provide air flow without worrying about creating a breathy tone as long as it is in concert with the Open Body. This should be a comforting thought to the singer who worries about breathiness.

If a singer tends toward too much abdominal tension (as in the piano-moving state), it would be good to go in the other direction for a while by exaggerating abdominal flexibility, until the proper balance can be achieved. However, the erect posture and expanded rib cage should remain intact. The abdominals participate in the process of judiciously providing air flow, especially noticeable in louder singing and with percussive effects. However, this is often exaggerated, creating too much force in singing. A flexible balance between the muscles of inhalation and the abdominal muscles can manage air flow well without unregulated force.

Part 4: Resonating on Spoken Tones

The next step is to phonate and resonate while maintaining the buoyant openness in both the body and the throat. This might sound too simple, but given that it is an integrative task rather than an isolated task, it may need a more conscious approach than what might first be assumed. Be assured that while maintaining the position of expansion is a learned skill, providing air to phonate is often relatively instinctive.

Phonating in an expansive body is often experienced more like inhalation than exhalation and for very physical reasons. The muscles that control the expulsion of air are predominantly those used for inhalation. Said another way, the muscles of inhalation are the muscles of expansion, are the muscles of breath management. These muscles serve the Open Throat of good resonance.

Before the singing voice is employed, the principles of resonance are applied to the speaking voice. Eliminating the pitch factor, as well as any preconceived notions about tone quality in the singing voice, clears the way for focusing on the Open Body/Open Throat as the primary enablers of good resonance. This is applicable to singing.

Although most people have less than perfectly resonating speaking voices, when they are instructed how to speak with an Open Body and Open Throat, improvement in the tonal quality is easy to hear. It is the difference between the everyday speaking voice and what might be called a "stage voice." The stage voice is a fuller, richer, more voluminous voice that is achieved with better breath management and resonance. A richly resonated speaking voice enabled by the Open Body and Open Throat can serve as a conduit to a well-resonated singing voice.

EXERCISE

This exercise begins with vowel sounds, primarily the sounds of "aw," "ay" (without a diphthong though), "ee," "oh," and "oo." They will be indicated by IPA symbols: "aw" = [ɑ], "ay" = [e], "ee" = [i], "oh" = [o], and "oo" = [u]. These are the five most common vowel sounds used in vocalises for singers. (See the appendix for a list of selected IPA symbols.)

- With a loosely dropped jaw, take the complete breath, creating both the Open Body and the Open Throat. Hold it for a second or two for consciousness raising to establish the sensations of postural alignment and expansion.

Trap: It is common, even in advanced singers, that this expanded position falters when phonation begins. At that moment, beginners may tend to collapse, and more advanced singers may lockset the body. (This is, of course, a generalization.) Although these problems begin in the breathing muscles, they result in manipulative control in the throat, something I have earlier coined as "throat support," a poor substitute for breath control. It is counterproductive to free resonance.

As you begin to phonate, remember that as long as the body maintains its lift, you can move the breath freely without it being excessive.

- Next, without disturbing the open position of body and throat and using a sustained tone, speak [ɑ] [e] [i] [o] [u] on one flow of the breath.
- Even though no particular pitch is used, think of the tone as being one continuous tone, not five separate tones. The vowels should not in any way stop or hinder the flow of the tone. One should seamlessly morph into the other.

Trap: If the pharyngeal space or body expansion either relaxes or locksets, another try or two should correct that tendency, and the difference in tone will be apparent. The goal is to maintain the Open Body and Open Throat while speaking. Don't skip the step of consciousness raising before beginning to phonate. The resulting tone should be distinctly different from the daily speaking tone. Make sure that the tongue movement that forms the vowels is facilitated loosely. If after several tries you feel as though the vowels are not as freely resonating as they might be, drop the jaw a bit farther. Dropping the jaw demands more independence of the tongue in the formation of vowels and discourages impingement on throat space. Such independence of the tongue and other articulators is the thrust of the discussion of the Third Step, Forward Articulation, in chapter 5.

- Take care not to use extraneous jaw or lip movements for the vowels. Use only movements that are needed to form the vowels. Note that [ɑ] [e] and [i] require no change of mouth position, only tongue position. Only [o] and [u] require a change of lip position, the pursing of the lips. A consistent quality of unimpeded resonance should flow through all five vowel sounds. More on that in chapter 5.

Part 5: Resonating on Sung Tones

The next step is to phonate and resonate sung tones on a sustained pitch. The pitch on the treble staff is a mere suggestion. The singer should choose the most comfortable pitch in the middle range, wherever that is. You can try the exercises on different pitches and observe the results, but please don't stray from the middle of your range yet.

As with most exercises in this book, these consist of two parts: the physical setup and a simple vocalization. The physical setup prepares the vocalization for a complete kinesthetic experience. To sing the vocalizations, though rudimentary, with beautiful resonance that results from an Open Throat built on an Open Body is no small accomplishment. Simplicity of approach can teach much about the kinesthetic experience of singing with the body–throat connection that enables good resonance. This is true for the beginner who is searching for a voice, as well as for the more advanced singer who is trying to root out a problem or find freer resonance. Building a firm foundation prepares the way for building more refined skills, to be addressed in part III.

The next exercise consists of five vowels sung on one sustained tone. Figure 4.1 presents this in conventional notation. The notation in figure 4.2 is more reflective of a single, continuous tone with five vowels, and it is the one you should model as you do this exercise.

[a]   [e]   [i]   [o]   [u]

Figure 4.1.   Five vowels conventionally notated.

[a   e   i   o   u]

Figure 4.2.   Continuous resonance on five vowels.

Figure 4.2 utilizes what is known as a *breve,* a single note that should be sustained for as long as it takes to sing the five vowel sounds. Notating the exercise in this way, while a bit unconventional, reflects the nature of a properly sustained tone on vowels. The shifts of tongue position required of the vowels need not interfere with the sustained and consistent flow of tone. It is similar to the violinist's bow making a single, long bowing on one string while the left hand makes pitch changes. The single long bowing is equivalent to the singer's even flow of breath. The pitches made on the violin are equivalent to sung vowels; they are resonance adjustments of a continuous tone. Vowels impart different colors to the tone but should maintain consistently free and full resonance.

EXERCISE

- Before attempting to sing the vocalization of Figure 4.2, make the preparations for the kinesthetic experience of good resonance (parts 1–3).
- Make sure you spend a moment or two on the singer's expanded position, and do not let it falter as you begin to phonate. Remember that this is a crucial juncture that demands heightened awareness.
- Sing [a] [e] [i] [o] [u] on one continuous pitch of your choice in your middle range. As in the speaking exercise, do not allow interruptions of tone between the vowels. Sing these notes as a single tone on which the five vowel sounds are seamlessly superimposed on it, rather than as five separate notes. Let each vowel seamlessly morph into the next.
- Be sure that the tongue movements are as far forward as possible and that they do not impinge on the throat space.

- Use a slow tempo to allow time to mentally observe the body and throat, making sure that they are working as a unit. It is important to focus on the physicality of the exercise rather than on the tone so that you do not attempt any throat manipulation in an effort to please your ear. If the tone is served well by the body, the tone will be of good quality.
- When you achieve some success at your starting pitch, move the exercise up and down a few steps, but stay in your middle range for now.

Only after you have focused on the Open Body/Open Throat and have found success with that should you place your attention on the actual tone. You should hear a consistently free, clear, and warm tone throughout all five vowels without any obvious change of quality other than what is necessary to form the vowels. Some singers who experience full and free resonance for the first time often comment with some dismay that they don't hear the tone anymore! The reason for this is that free tones escape the body. The ear hears tense, trapped tones much better than free ones. Other singers who experience a fuller and richer tone immediately find it rewarding. I've never quite figured out why the reactions differ so widely to the same phenomenon—other than there are no two singers alike!

If the quality of tone seems to be lacking after the preparatory breath, most likely it is due to a body in collapse, push, or lockset. Increased efforts of expansion should help curb any of these tendencies and assist in breath management. By maintaining the lift of the body and the Open Throat, air is always easily accessible, and the singer can control how much air is needed for any given musical situation. There is no control in collapse and no free air flow in lockset. Although the kinesthetic experience requires work in the body, especially in the rib muscles and in the diaphragm, good resonance feels free and easy in the throat.

The goal for the exercises in this chapter is for the singer to experience the direct relationship between the body's work and resonance. All singing skills, including those with greater refinements, are built on this relationship.

The next exercise introduces a consonant. The humming [m] is used in many traditionally sound-teaching methods as a helpful way of "placing" the voice (a separate discussion), but there are as many or more incorrect ways of making the [m] as correct ways. All are not equal.

Although forming the [m] may appear to be an insignificant increase of complexity, like other consonants it requires special consideration. For example, rather than an open jaw used in the pure vowel sounds, the singer now has to close the mouth for each [m]. Singers often tense their lips to make the consonant when all that is needed is for the lips to be loosely touching one another. When there is tension in the lip area, tension in the mouth and throat may very well accompany it, resulting in constricted resonating cavities. The result is a loss of resonance on the [m], and this may negatively affect preceding or subsequent vowels. Even though the exit of the air for the nasal [m] is through the nose rather than the mouth, the mouth and throat should retain as much resonating space as possible behind the lips.

EXERCISE

To minimize the tendency to lose space in the mouth cavity or throat, the vocalization in figure 4.3a places an [ɑ] before and after each [m]. Unconventional notation is used again to indicate the continuity of the resonance through both vowel and consonant. The goal for these exercises is to match the resonance quality of vowel and pitched consonant as much as possible.

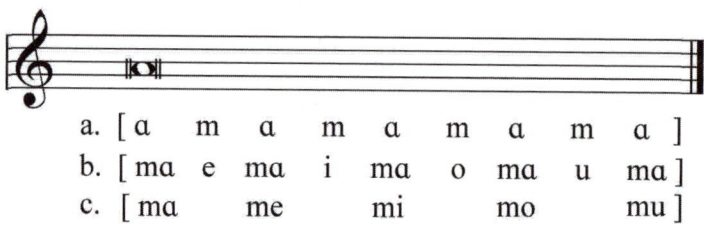

Figure 4.3.   **Introducing a consonant.**

- For the vocalization of Figure 4.3a, choose a comfortable pitch in your middle range.
- Prepare the singer's body, loosely drop the jaw, and take an expansive breath. Pause a bit before singing to increase your awareness of the body's expansion and to begin the tone with a gentle and subtle flow of air without losing any lift of the body.
- The tongue should be loosely lying at the bottom of the mouth for the [ɑ]. When moving into the [m], loosely place the lips together in front of the [ɑ] space without diminishing that space. Maintain the lift of the body as you morph from the vowel to the consonant, and keep in mind that the [m], called a semivowel, is a fully sustainable consonant that can be well resonated. Allot equal time to both vowel and consonant.
- Slowly alternate between the [ɑ] and [m], giving the vowel and humming consonant consistent resonance and even flow while maintaining the Open Body and Open Throat.
- When you achieve some success on your starting pitch, move the exercise up and down a few steps, but stay in your middle range for now.

EXERCISE

In figure 4.3b and 4.3c, four other vowels are added to the vocalization. They require the tongue to become more active. It lifts toward the front for the [e] and [i] (farther forward for the [i]) and toward the back for the [o] and [u] (farther back for the [u]). In forming these vowels, do not insert extraneous tension into the tongue or any part of the mouth. The lift of tongue can be accomplished loosely and comfortably. (Remember the example of lifting my arm with and without tension. Without tension is better.)

In figure 4.3b, rather than using the [m] as an independent sound, it is combined with a vowel to form the syllable [m ɑ]. Although this requires moving through the [m] more quickly than in figure 4.3a, it must not lose any resonating space. The resonance potential of the [m] combined with the open [ɑ] makes it a good model for the rest of the vowels. As you move from syllable to vowel, minimize the movements of the articulators so that they do no more than necessary to achieve the correct vowel sound. The tongue movements should be executed loosely and as forward as possible so as not to impinge on the throat space.

- Choose a pitch in your middle range. Prepare the singer's body, loosely drop the jaw as if you are about to sing an [ɑ], and take an expansive breath. Pause a bit before singing to increase your awareness of the body's expansion, and begin the tone without losing any lift of the body.
- With the tongue loosely lying at the bottom of the mouth, place the lips together to prepare for the [m ɑ].
- Continually and actively lift the body as you move through the vocalization. This is to counteract the natural tendency to relax the body's expansion, push, or lockset the position.
- The air-filled cavities that resonate the vowels and consonant should maintain a similar spaciousness while the vowels elicit changes of tone color.

Trap: The [e] and [i] often have a tendency to sound thin or "white," usually because the articulation invades the throat space in more or less degree. This is often accompanied with a spread of the mouth despite the fact that no change of mouth or jaw position is needed for these vowels, only tongue position.

Sing a single, uninterrupted, and sustainable tone throughout the vocalization, as expressed by the single breve note in figure 4.3b.

When you achieve some success on this pitch, move the exercise up and down a few steps, but stay in your middle range for now.

EXERCISE

In figure 4.3c, the [m] precedes each vowel, forming five syllables. The air flow for the nasal [m] goes up through the nasopharynx, the highest section of the pharynx, the top of the vocal tract. The singer's experience of height on the [m] is therefore very real. As you flow from the consonant through each vowel, try to maintain some of that height.

- Prepare the singer's body. In taking the breath with a loosely dropped jaw, open spaces as you would for singing an [a]. Retain that space as you close the lips for each [m] and for each vowel that follows. The tongue's movements should be loose but distinct enough so that the vowels are clearly identifiable.
- Form all your vowels in a vertical framework aided by a loosely dropped jaw and with no spread of the mouth position.
- Sing one continuous tone throughout with consistent resonance and an even flow of breath.
- When you achieve some success on this pitch, move the exercise up and down a few steps, but stay in your middle range for now.

Working with the [m] has been a gentle but important introduction to consonants, some of which entail a good deal more challenge. The articulation of most consonants should not cause any constriction in the resonating cavities. The next chapter on articulation addresses this in much more detail.

TALKING POINTS

This chapter has focused on the most important elements of creating receptive resonance spaces for beautiful and free singing. While the Three-Step Approach has a particular style, I believe that most of the assumptions underlying it are not particularly controversial.

However, there are some issues on which it might be more difficult to find consensus. They may be matters of taste, preference, or terminology and tend to elicit a variety of opinions and perspectives. They are familiar topics to most teachers and singers. They can be either peripheral or central to the development of a vocal technique. How they are addressed affects the teacher's style and the singer's concepts. These talking points include the following:

- Whether we seek a tone that is forward or back or a combination of both, as well as the issue of "placing the voice."
- Whether the timbre to be sought is dark or bright or a combination of both.
- Whether the pharyngeal space (Open Throat) should be more focused on width or height.
- What the best positions are for the soft palate (the upper back of the mouth) and how they should be approached.

- How much nasality is good in a tone and whether it should have any presence in non-nasal vowels.
- How much mouth opening is needed and how it affects tone, depending on vowel, pitch, and volume.
- How the tongue affects resonance, especially with regard to articulation.

These are all relevant and detailed topics for a discussion of vocal technique. Some of them have been either directly or indirectly referred to earlier. However, since this is a "doing book," discussion has primarily served the purpose of giving context to exercises that foster kinesthetic experience. There is always room for broader discussion about singing. The following talking points address some terminologies, concerns, and issues in a larger pedagogic framework and show how the Three-Step Approach addresses them.

Forward/Back

One of the more sensitive issues of singing and teaching has to do with the forward/back polarities. A rather commonly accepted belief is that the tone must be "placed forward." The traditional instruction to "sing in the mask" is an example of imagery that has a long history and is still commonly used in voice studios today. Although it seems to be well respected and often used, exactly what is meant by the term is not always clear.

Efforts to bring the tone forward are part of a "placement" theory of singing. This imagery implies that one can somehow guide the tone forward to gain clarity and ring and that doing so prevents muffled or "throaty" tones. The goals of "placement" are to produce a free, ringing tone with no hint of the throat in it. This is not to be challenged by the Three-Step Approach. However, one has to question the methods to facilitate forward placement by asking what physical parts guide the tone "forward" and even what "forward" means.

Forward Articulation, the third of the Three-Step Approach, has a different meaning than "placing the voice forward," although it might be somewhat related. Forward Articulation refers specifically to the physical properties and function of articulators such as the mouth, tongue, and soft palate. Forward Articulation discourages unnecessary involvement of the throat and allows unhampered air flow. In contrast, the emphasis for "placing the voice forward" is on vocal sound. It is an extremely elusive directive with no specificity regarding just how the singer is supposed to do that. Although this example of imagery is a time-honored one, it does not address the physicality necessary to produce the desired "forward tone."

The association of forward voice placement with the "mask" area is a bit more puzzling. The mask area is roughly the area of the sinuses. The moist sinuses do not act as good resonators of the voice. Therefore, singing "in the mask" must not mean resonating "in the mask." Furthermore, ring is likely created in the larynx, the lower portion of the pharynx, which is a significant distance away from "the mask."

Forward placement could also refer to the mouth area, since the mouth is considered to be the forward resonator that enhances a bright timbre. However, tones that are primarily resonated in the mouth lack pharyngeal space and are often called "mouthy," "white," or "spread," none of which is complimentary.

In speaking of resonance in the context of forward placement, the role of the pharynx seems to be left out even though it is the largest resonator. The implication seems to be that the pharynx is somehow dangerous territory and that, if we mention it, we will call attention to it and use it in the wrong way, whereas if we don't mention it, it will be used correctly. To me, unlike training in other physical activities, it seems to avoid an issue rather than confront it directly.

Often the phrase "singing too far back" has been equated with "throaty" or "muffled" singing. Avoiding this may be the raison d'etre of teaching "forward placement," but avoiding the role of the pharynx seems to be limiting at best. The mind-set of the Three Steps is that the problem is not the open pharynx, which is a back resonator, but rather constriction in that area. The Open Throat contributes richness to the timbre, and the mouth contributes brightness. For a free and full resonance system, both polarities must function in a flexible balance.

I do not wish to negate all usefulness of the "forward placement" suggestion. I merely caution that forward placement must not minimize the pharyngeal (back) resonance that would enrich the tone and, at the same time, allow it to exit freely forward through the mouth cavity.

When full and free resonance is tapped, the singer often feels little or nothing in the throat. However, sympathetic vibrations in various parts of the body might be experienced as a buzz of sorts in the hard palate area, the lips, the teeth, the nose, or the "mask." For lower tones, this buzz might be felt in the chest. But these sensations do not create resonance; they are a result of it.

Dark or Light: *The* Chiaroscuro *Balance*

The balance between forward and back allows light and dark, bright and rich qualities in a tone. The Italian term for this balance of contrasting tonal elements is *chiaroscuro*. It might be considered to be the sine qua non of beautiful resonance.

One often hears the criticism that a singer's voice is too dark, but one rarely hears the criticism that it is too rich. They both have to do with the pharynx. Rather than perceiving a tone as "too dark," it might be more apt to think of it as not having enough "brightness" and vice versa. A full spectrum of resonance includes as much dark as possible and as much light as possible.

Pharyngeal Space

You may be asking whether the throat space should be longer vertically or wider horizontally. The answer would have to be "Yes!" The size and shape of the pharynx are not rigid. It is dynamic and flexible, changing shape constantly depending on factors such as pitch, volume, and vowel. Although there may be an ideal theoretical dimension for each vowel and each pitch in the scale, the singer is not able to operate the pharynx with that kind of machine-like precision. However, with a stable low larynx, a spacious and flexible pharynx is quite capable of adjusting to whatever pitch, volume, and vowel are sent through it.

You may recall from the phonation exercises that mention was made of the Adam's apple. This is the protruding notch in the front of the neck, usually more prominent in men than women, which roughly indicates where the vocal folds are attached to a laryngeal cartilage. In taking a yawning breath, this notch lowers as the larynx lowers. In this position, the pharyngeal column is lengthened vertically. The lowered larynx gives the throat a deeper spaciousness to it. Along with the lowered diaphragm, the instruction to "take a deep breath" is therefore physically relevant.

As with other issues in singing, the height/width matter is not an either/or situation. If the conditions in the body are correct, the adjustments of the resonators are rather automatic as long as the larynx stays low and the pharynx remains flexibly opened. However, keeping the larynx low, particularly as the pitch rises, takes considerable intentionality and requires more energy from the Open Body. Approaching the upper range is addressed more thoroughly in chapter 7.

Excessive lowering of the larynx is not necessary and would disallow appropriate width, and excessive width would disallow appropriate height. In either case, excessiveness is to be avoided in favor of flexibility served by an Open Body.

For the singer new to the experience of enhanced pharyngeal space, the sensation of more width in the pharyngeal area is just as significant as the sensation of depth and probably does not feel comfortable at first. As the singer progresses, the throat may achieve its potential for flexible width, and the vertical dimensions might become more important. (It could work the other way around as well.) Verticality is associated with the lowered diaphragm and larynx, spacious air-filled throat, and dropped jaw with no spread of the mouth position. It is important in finding ring in the voice, avoiding a spread tone, and singing comfortably in the upper range. It becomes more and more important in the chapters of part III, which address refinements of singing technique.

When I've asked a singer how a new and improved resonant sound feels, instead of the expected answer of "rich" or "big" (which I hear in the sound), the answer is often "free." Although this is not what I'm expecting, it is a good answer, indeed! The voice is full and rich *because* it is free. The verbal prompts to achieve are not "sing rich," "sing big," "sing free," or "sing forward" but rather "Open Body/Open Throat" and all that is implied by that.

Soft Palate

The height of the vertical vocal tract touches on matters of the soft palate. Behind the hard palate (the roof of the mouth just behind the teeth) lies the soft palate. As the name implies, it is a soft area, and when you look in a mirror, you might see a little extension hanging down from it in the back. This, you may know, is the uvula. The main importance of the soft palate in singing is that it is flexible and, therefore, an omnipresent factor in resonance, for good or bad. It is also particularly active in regulating the amount of nasality in the tone, but this function is addressed separately in the next section.

Often, you hear voice teachers and singers talk about lifting the soft palate. Many fine teachers believe that lifting the soft palate provides a sensation of height in the throat column, either literally or as an image. I think most would agree that singers need to sense much height in the vocal tract while singing. However, trying to intentionally lift it might be difficult to do with any precision and could conceivably create unnecessary tension there. The yawning breath (actually the preyawn breath) might accomplish much the same thing without a specific instruction to lift the soft palate.

The Three-Step Approach assumes that the soft palate most often does what it needs to do when the unit of the Open Body, Open Throat, and Forward Articulation is working well and there are no extraneous tensions in the vocal tract. When the unit is not functioning correctly, excessive rigidity can pop up anywhere, including the soft palate, in an effort to compensate.

Excessive rigidity in the soft palate area, something I call "clutching," is almost like a cramp in the soft palate area. The clutching soft palate is tense and to some degree low. It creates a rigid "roof" on the vocal tract, limiting the experience of height or flexibility there. As with most dysfunctions, the singer is not clutching on purpose but only as a substitute for something else that is not working. Inadequate breath management is often the culprit behind the clutched soft palate, especially a squeeze or push in the body. It results in a muffled, tense sound with garbled vowels. This limits the throat's receptivity as a resonator and is likely to cause pitch problems as well as a constricted tone. It often indicates an effort, conscious or not, to control the breath in the throat.

Clutching in the soft palate easily could extend down the throat, causing a glottal attack of the tone. A glottal attack is percussive, the result of air being forced through vocal folds that have been pressed together after inhalation. Of course, this is antithetical to free tone flow and should be avoided. More desirable is a gentle onset of tone initiated with a free flow of breath.

A clutched soft palate often makes an [ɑ] sound like [ʌ] as in "fun," with muscle involvement being apparent. The problem is not with the vowel itself but with the soft palate. The [ʌ] can be sung quite legitimately, loosely formed without the negative effects of a rigid soft palate. This is discussed more in chapter 5, on articulation.

Like any tension in the throat, a clutched soft palate makes the pharynx and mouth static rather than flexible. This is what causes pitch problems. If the resonance unit is not flexible, it cannot adjust to varying pitches. As mentioned previously, trying to put a tone through an unreceptive resonator is like trying to put a square peg in a round hole. It is usually not a problem of the ear but of the resonance receptacle. In my experience, once the singer gains more awareness of the soft palate area and its relationship to the Open Body/Open Throat, instruction to intentionally lift the soft palate is rarely necessary.

At the other extreme of a clutched soft palate is a soft palate that lifts so far up and back that it touches the back wall of the throat. When it moves that far, it completely shuts off the portal to the upper part of the pharynx, thereby eliminating the participation of nasal resonators. The amount of nasality in a tone depends on how high and how far back the soft palate is lifted. There is much debate as to exactly how much, if any, nasality is necessary in a good singing tone.

Many pedagogues believe that lifting the soft palate up and back is not only useful for preventing excessive nasality but should be employed to block all nasal quality in non-nasal vowels or consonants. Others question that assumption. Shutting off the taller, narrower portion of the pharynx eliminates some height in the vocal tract, something that is generally considered a positive thing.

Ring in the voice, which is characteristic of a fully resonant voice, has been identified pitchwise at approximately 2,800 frequencies per second, a pitch at the top end of the piano keyboard. Small cavities, as in the larynx, are receptive to higher frequencies. It is conceivable that the height and narrower width of the nasopharynx could contribute to ring. Whether it does or not, completely closing the nasal port for all singing might be missing an opportunity for more complexity in the resonance unit.

Well-respected pedagogies over centuries have used the [m] in front of various vowels, sometimes as a way of "placing the voice in the mask." This suggests that vowels were perceived to benefit from a close relationship to that nasal consonant and that retaining at least some of the nasopharynx involvement might enhance the vowel's tone. Might this be true of all vowels whether or not they follow a nasal consonant?

Although consensus has not been gained on exactly how far the soft palate should lift, consensus is easier to find on the view that the soft palate should not be so low as to result in muddy vowels or nasality that draws attention to itself. Neither a completely lax nor rigid soft palate serves resonance well.

Nasality

Excessive nasality is caused by a soft palate that is too low, by being either too lax or too rigid as in a "clutch." The entrance of the tonal stream into the mouth is blocked in more or less degree. Unable to freely enter and proceed out the mouth, the tone is diverted up behind the soft palate, through the upper portion of the pharynx (the nasopharynx), and out the nose. Most people agree that except for those consonants and vowels that are supposed to be nasal, as in the French language, undue nasality is not beautiful. Nasality that calls attention to itself is generally considered to be undue or excessive and certainly not beautiful. Since the soft palate is too low in nasal singing, it must be encouraged to lift either directly or indirectly. The Three-Step Approach would first assess the function of the Open Body/Open Throat and, only after resolving problems there, move to the soft palate directly if needed.

One exercise that directly focuses on the actions of the soft palate employs the [ŋ] in combination with a vowel, such as [ɑ], as in [ŋ] [ɑ] [ŋ] [ɑ] [ŋ] [ɑ]. (See the appendix.) Alternating between the two articulations highlights the range of movement in the soft palate. At one extreme is the [ŋ] position, which completely closes off the entrance to mouth cavity and diverts the tone solely through the nose. The [ɑ] releases that blockage as it assumes a rather relaxed, low-lying tongue. Quick alternations between the [ŋ] and [ɑ] encourage flexibility in the area with the soft palate and tongue. Most important, though, it helps the singer to develop meaningful awareness and control of the soft palate area as needed.

Plosive consonants placed before the vowel, such as [b] and [p], can also help to pop the soft palate up. This and other matters involving articulation and its relationship to resonance are covered in the following chapter.

Jaw/Mouth Opening

Relaxing the jaw can improve resonance quite quickly. The jaw should be as loose as possible, freely moving on its hinges where it attaches to the skull. Fluid adjustments of the jaw opening are needed to match the variety of pitches, vowels, consonants, and volume.

Working with the mouth and jaw opening may be easier to understand than working with the throat spaces just because of its visibility. But habit, which is an entity that has a life of its own, can rear its ugly head in any area involved in singing. Breaking a habit is much more difficult than learning the correct way to do something in the first place.

Some habits with the jaw occur by default; no other way has been learned. In such a case, the jaw is simply not dropping as much as needed for singing, or it has assumed some tension if the body is not doing its job. Habits involving tension are generally compensatory efforts of the singer when good breath management and resonance are lacking. However, since the healthy functioning of the singer's body has been well documented so far, I'll jump to other means of addressing problems of the jaw.

More often than not, the jaw is not dropped enough due to tension. When the jaw is tense, other parts of the vocal mechanism tense as well, in a chain of tensions. The jaw must be freed of undue tension for many reasons, not the least of which is that the deeply dropped jaw is needed in the upper ranges. Strangely enough, singers who are reticent about dropping their jaws readily accept watching great singers onstage whose jaws are often dropped deeply. (The jaw's role in high and loud singing is addressed more in part III.)

One way of attacking this directly is for the singer to place three fingers between the front teeth while singing the five vowels beginning with [ɑ]. Singers don't particularly like to do this because it upsets their current tensions, crutches that they have come to rely on, as counterproductive as that is. However, the three-finger routine provides the strongest "encouragement" I know of for eliciting independence of both the jaw and the articulators. It is a means toward a good end. If the throat opening has been either constricted or lax, the dropped jaw will help to create a good middle ground. By breaking one link in the chain of events, such as a tense jaw, other tensions are often disallowed as well.

A good general rule to follow is that the deeply dropped jaw must accompany high or loud singing. In other situations, it can take a more modified opening, but it must always be loose. This is discussed in detail in chapter 7, on developing the upper range.

Tongue Involvement

The tongue is a major articulator of vowels and many consonants. Articulation is discussed in detail in the next chapter, but what is important here is that vowels and consonants are not just word makers; they are major resonance adjusters. This is especially true of the tongue's formations of vowels.

While clarity is important, the muscle movements of good articulation should not interfere with the open pharynx, nor should they impede the loosely dropped jaw. This might involve some vowel modification in the higher ranges.

The biggest problem with the tongue is that without adequate body preparation and good breath management, it tends to pull back. This directly impedes throat space. Manipulations of the tongue and throat take over, and the tension results in a muffled or strident tone with indistinct articulation. The Three-Step Approach addresses this primarily through the kinesthetic experience of proper breath management and articulation. Using consonants that exercise the tongue such as [l] [t] and [ð] is helpful in bringing awareness and flexibility to the tongue.

SUMMARY

This chapter addresses the basics of resonance, how it can be enhanced, and how undue tensions and constrictions can inhibit it. Full resonance depends on the Open Throat, and the Open Throat depends on the Open Body. The buoyantly expanded body manages the breath as the first step in creating a refined tone. The flexible air-filled cavities of pharynx, mouth, and nose sympathetically resonate with the pitch and vowel, thereby enhancing the tone. The result is a well-grounded, beautiful, voluminous, and flexible voice that can abundantly express itself in song and aria.

Voices that function in the fullness of their instrument will be satisfying to the listener and will have the capability of expressing emotion through music in ways that less complete voices cannot. A singer who is not singing in the fullness of the instrument, with either a small voice or a large voice, will have less impact on the listener even though the instrument itself might be very special. A voice that includes the full spectrum of uninhibited resonance might be called "organic," "authentic," and "immediate." It is more connected to the singer's whole body and, I would say, to a musical soul as well.

Singers work hard to interpret and project the drama of the text and music, as well they should. But the expressive impact of a fully resonating voice has a power all of its own. Such an uninhibited voice reflects a mere thought held by the singer. The joy of singing with a free voice is immeasurable, as any singer who has experienced this will attest. The freely resonating voice is what keeps singers going back to the practice room. It is the singer's Holy Grail!

The next chapter, on Forward Articulation, is the third of the OOFing steps. It explores the articulation of words in relationship to consistent resonance. Adding Forward Articulation to the Open Body and Open Throat brings the integrative nature of the Three Steps full circle.

Step 3: "Forward Articulation" and Enunciation

$\mathscr{T}$he Three-Step Approach employing the OOFing mantra as a focal point began with a discussion of the Open Body as it relates to good breath management, and it proceeded to the Open Throat as it relates to good resonance. Forward Articulation is the third step, and its importance lies not only in clear enunciation but in its relationship to the Open Body and Open Throat. As another participator in resonance, it is now both layered onto and integrated with the other two steps. As such, this discussion treats clear enunciation and good resonance as inseparable in a good vocal technique.

Articulation is the process of forming intelligible vowels and consonants giving rise to words and, in turn, text. The articulators, such as the tongue, lips, jaw, and soft palate, each have a specific role to play in the process. Their precise positioning determines the vowels and consonants that are sounded. If a singer is trying to make the vowel sound "oh" but does not place the tongue and lips in the right position, a vowel sound other than "oh" will be voiced.

As with good breath management and enunciation, articulation requires some degree of muscle work, but the articulators must be free to do their job without undue tension. Any kind of rigidity in the articulators hinders their movements and, therefore, clarity of enunciation. It also impinges on the throat, thereby limiting the potential for full resonance. Conversely, if there is rigidity elsewhere in the body, both resonance and articulation are likely to be negatively affected.

As mentioned in the last chapter, Forward Articulation is not to be confused with "forward placement." Forward Articulation is physically definable. It identifies the physical parts that must function as forward as possible so that pharyngeal resonance is not hindered. My choice of terms reflects the primary goals of the Three-Step Approach, namely to use the clearest, most definable terminology possible, all of which relate to the physical and kinesthetic experience of singing.

Forward Articulation that functions simultaneously with the Open Throat in back is an example of the polarities that coexist in singing. Many vowels and consonants are easily articulated in front of the throat. If the articulator movements are kept forward, rich resonance enabled in an Open Throat can remain unimpaired. Combined with the light/bright resonance produced by the mouth cavity, the singer's fullest resonance spectrum can be tapped. Clear articulation can be achieved in a consistent *chiaroscuro* tonal palette.

The clear articulation of words in full resonance might feel very different from what is experienced in everyday speaking. As a daily habit, most people do not make an effort to speak either with precise clarity or beautiful resonance unless involved in a public presentation of some kind for which a more conscious attention to quality might be needed. Some fortunate singers have naturally resonant speaking voices, very near the quality of their singing voices. For others, even excellent singers, the speaking voice and singing voice are often miles apart, and this can be problematic. It can mean that the singer's unit of Open Body, Open Throat, and Forward Articulation is not as familiar and natural as it could be.

When I work with singers whose speaking voice is significantly lacking in quality, I suggest a more conscious approach to their vocal production in speech. This means speaking with better breath management and a more intentional opening in the throat, just as with singing. As demonstrated in the last chapter, this produces the resonant quality of the "stage voice." It is usually relatively easy to achieve with singers who are well familiarized with the mechanics of their vocal instrument. However, to make it a new habit for everyday use in speaking is much more difficult and takes commitment. With greater awareness and practice, though, the speaking voice can improve and positively contribute to the muscle memory needed for singing. This makes the cultivated sound of fine singing and the kinesthetic experiences that create it more natural and therefore easier to access.

An improved speaking quality can serve as a model for good singing quality, a tactic used in the last chapter in first approaching the kinesthetic experience of full resonance. This process can also be reversed, as when a speech therapist or laryngologist suggests singing lessons as a first step in therapy. It can work both ways.

THE CONTEXT

Before we begin the exercises in this chapter, it is important to understand the relationship between articulation and resonance. Vowels and consonants are determined by characteristic adjustments of the articulators, and these adjustments affect resonance. Therefore, to provide the context for the exercises, an overview of vowels and consonants is in order.

The IPA (International Phonetic Alphabet) will be helpful in this discussion. It is a collection of bracketed symbols, each representing a specific sound of language. One sound might be heard in one language only, another in many languages. The five vowel sounds often used by English-speaking singers in vocalises are something like "ah," "ay," "ee," "oh," and "oo." Those sounds are represented respectively by the following IPA symbols: [ɑ] [e] [i] [o] [u]. There are many variations of these basic vowels. For instance, the letter *a* in the word *hat* is not one of the basic five vowels but lies somewhere between the "ah" and "ay" and is represented by the IPA symbol [æ]. Or, the letter *i* in the word *bit* is not one of the five, and it is represented by the IPA symbol of [ɪ]. A selected list of IPA symbols, including those that represent consonants, is found in the appendix. Note that the symbols for consonants often, but not always, appear to be the same as letters in the English alphabet. For the sake of clarity and convenience, IPA symbols are used from now on whenever a vowel or consonant is being discussed.

Vowels

Vowels are unrestricted carriers of tone. Articulators form shapes in the resonating cavities that produce the many vowel sounds of language. The result is that resonance assumes a variety of timbres or colors. This is what makes enunciation clear, but it also is a source for much expressive potential. Despite the ever-changing palette of tone colors, consistently free and full resonance can be maintained. Forward Articulation ensures that the movements of articulation will not impinge on the Open Throat, a major source of rich resonance.

With an Open Throat and Open Body, Forward Articulation makes it possible to superimpose vowels—even bright vowels—on a rich tone. Some singers muddy vowels in a misplaced effort for a richer tone. These singers are not yet comfortable with the polarities of the Open Throat in back and articulation in front. It causes their coaches to ask for brighter vowels, a reasonable request. The singers will most likely acquiesce to that request but often forget about the Open Body and Open Throat in the process. This robs the tone of pharyngeal resonance and allows mouth resonance to dominate, thereby creating "white" tones. Because the vowel is no longer artificially darkened and therefore clearer, the coach might be somewhat satisfied with it. However, while a "white" vowel may be clearer than a muddy one, the trade-off with resonance is not a good option. A white tone is thin, starved of richness, and lacking luster. A better option is for the bright vowel to maintain clarity through better tongue positioning while utilizing the rich resonance provided by the Open Throat and the Open Body. This is the best of both worlds!

Since one of the goals of this book is to simplify the process of singing through simpler terminology, I feel somewhat justified to offer one of my more homespun analogies for the function of the articulators. There are some similarities, although partial, between the templates placed on the front of a baker's cookie press and articulation. (I appreciate that some of the more science-minded readers might feel compelled to skip this part, but I'll proceed anyway.) The cookie press is often shaped somewhat like a gun with a barrel, handle, and trigger, and it is used to form decorative shapes out of cookie dough. (Many young students have never seen one, but they do remember their Play-Doh toys!) The dough is fed through the barrel by the trigger on the handle. It exits through a template with a cutout design of a wreath, animal, Christmas tree, or some other shape. The template is placed at the end of the barrel. When the trigger is squeezed, the dough is fed through the barrel with a well-managed even flow. The template forms the exiting dough into the shape dictated by its cutout design. If the template is changed, the cookie shape is changed. The analogy loosely compares the function of the barrel to the throat, the dough to the movement of resonating air, and the trigger to the management of breath flow. Most important, and closest to the actuality of vowel shaping, it compares vowel making to the function of the templates. In effect, the shapes created by the articulators, particularly the tongue, are templates that give rise to specific vowels and the resonance properties associated with them. Each vowel is the product of a specific template. I have found that for those singers who are familiar with a cookie press (or at least the Play-Doh apparatus), this can be an uncomplicated but meaningful *Ah-ha!* moment.

While some vowels are considered forward vowels and others back vowels, they all should be as forward as possible, not impinging on a flexible Open Throat behind them. The tongue should be as relaxed as possible, even while moving to varying positions in the mouth. When most lax, the tongue lies loosely at the bottom of the mouth, with the tip gently touching the inside of the front-bottom teeth. If this seems to require effort, it is probably an indication of tension in the tongue, particularly if the tongue is lifting or pulling back in the mouth. This is addressed later in the chapter.

As you experiment with speaking the vowels addressed here, be sure you prepare for it as a singer, with an Open Body and Open Throat. Otherwise, you will not find full resonance. By integrating the Three Steps in speech, doing so in singing will be easier. The vocal instrument is the same for both.

The [ɑ].   Aside from a more neutral vowel sound, the [ɑ] as in *water* is one of the more relaxed positions of the five vowel sounds, with the tongue lying low in the mouth as described earlier. The jaw should be loose and dropped. In working with the jaw, teachers often use the term "dumb jaw" to suggest a more relaxed opening. Similarly, the relaxed tongue might be called the "dumb tongue," as opposed to a tense tongue, which may be pulling up or back. Sometimes I suggest that the tongue should assume the lax state of a raw piece of liver, not a particularly beautiful thought, but it does give the impression of an amorphous blob!

The lips should not have any involvement other than being relaxed and showing a bit of upper teeth. Most mouths reveal a bit of upper teeth quite naturally when slightly open and completely relaxed. If the upper teeth are not showing, it means that the singer is inserting tension into the lips that is extraneous to the [ɑ].

The [e].   For the [e], as in *ba̱be*, the tongue needs to lift in the mouth. While the tip remains loosely lying at the bottom of the mouth, with the tongue touching the inside of the bottom teeth, the sides of the tongue at midpoint will need to rise and touch the upper molars. If you say the word *bay* repeatedly and quickly, most likely your tongue will go to the right position for the [e]. While doing this, make a mental note of that tongue position, as you will need to replicate it when singing it.

Of course, any tongue movement requires activated muscle, but remember that muscle action should be only as much as needed and executed with ease. As you may recall from an earlier discussion on tension, I contrasted moving my arm with and without tension. While both efforts brought the arm to the same position, it is clear that the tension was not necessary and that it worked against the movement. The position of the tongue for the [e], and for any other vowel, must be achieved with ease.

The [e] and [i] are considered bright vowels. They are often susceptible to undue throat involvement that can make them thin and tight. Involving the throat unnecessarily diminishes throat space, robbing the vowels of the rich quality that is possible. If articulated as forward as possible, the Open Throat will be free to produce its characteristic dark quality along with the bright quality of the [e] and [i].

The [i].   As with the [e], the [i] requires a lifting movement of the tongue. However, the lifting will be slightly more forward than that of the [e], and the sides of the tongue will rise farther forward and touch nearer the upper eye teeth. If you say the word *bee* repeatedly and quickly, most likely your tongue will go to the right position for the [i]. Make mental note of where the tongue touches the teeth, as you will need to replicate that when singing. The tip of the tongue should stay low, loosely touching the inside of the bottom front teeth but not forced there.

The [e] and [i] are known as "front" vowels because the lift of the tongue is relatively forward and the vowels have a bright color to them. This is as opposed to what are called the "back" vowels, the [o] and [u], for which the back part of the tongue lifts rather than the front part. The tongue lifts a little higher and farther back for the [u] than for the [o]. Back vowels possess a darker color than front vowels. Keep in mind that both back and front vowels can be well resonated in a spacious and flexible Open Throat.

The [o].   The [o] requires not only tongue movement but lip rounding as well. To find a relaxed rounding as well as the proper vowel sound, I suggest repeating [b o][b o] [b o] [b o] quickly and noting how loose the lips and tongue can be while achieving clear syllables. Be sure not to *squeeze* your lips together for the [b]. This is simply unnecessary tension. The lips need only to lie loosely together, gently and momentarily offering some resistance to the air passing through them. I use this consonant with the [o] because it discourages exaggerated opening of the lips for that vowel, especially when in the middle or low pitch ranges.

Because the [o] requires a lift at the back of the tongue, the tip might tend to pull back, but try to maintain it at a loose, low, forward position. As you speak the [b o] syllables, you might want to sustain the [o] at the end of a syllable so that you can spend some time with that shape and sound. Notice how little mouth opening you need for a closed [o]. Be sure to maintain the Open Body and Open Throat throughout the vocalizations that follow, or you will not achieve full resonance. While the throat will flex relative to the change of tongue position, it should remain flexibly open while the tongue and lips make their adjustments.

The [u].   The [u], as in *too*, is similar in color and shape as the [o], but the lift of the tongue is still higher and farther back, and the opening between the lips is slightly smaller. Nevertheless, notice how loose the lips can be in this position. Although the [u] is called a "closed" vowel, don't let that word equate to any closure of pharyngeal space. The often-used analogy to the inverted megaphone is particularly relevant to the formation of the [o] and [u]. The wide end of the megaphone relates to the Open Throat, and the narrow end relates to the rather closed position of the mouth, the point being that the closed position of the mouth and the open position of the throat can coexist to provide both clear enunciation and full resonance.

All other vowel sounds are slight variations of these basic positions. Even though certain resonance properties change with the vowel, the Open Throat and Open Body are stabilizers that allow consistent tone quality. In this chapter, vowel exercises are always integrated with good resonance.

Consonants

Consonants surround vowels, making syllables that form words. Unlike vowels, which have unrestricted air flow, consonants have varying degrees of air flow restriction. Some consonants are beautifully sustainable, and some are complete stoppages of the tone.

Some sustainable consonants are called semivowels because they can contribute to the steady flow of tone as well as vowels. They require only a minimum amount of air restriction and can sustain pitch. Even beyond their use for good enunciation, they can be valuable assets in singing a *legato* line and, as such, should be viewed as gifts to the singer. This is discussed more in part III.

The semivowels that have the most potential for contributing to a flowing vocal line are the [m] [n] and [ŋ]. (See the appendix.) The [m] requires closed lips; the [n] requires the tongue to touch the upper mouth just behind the upper front teeth; and the [ŋ] requires the tongue to lift and touch the back roof of the mouth. In each case, the exit of the breath occurs through the nose rather than the mouth. Therefore, they are called nasal consonants.

The upper throat behind the nose (the nasopharynx) becomes a primary passageway for the nasal consonants, one that is not used as much in nonnasal vowels and consonants. This resonating passageway and the nose itself lend a distinct quality to the tone that is identifiably nasal in quality. Although these nasal consonants prevent the tone from exiting the mouth, they should nevertheless have their full due of resonance. Although the air restriction is minimal, there is always the danger of impinging on resonator space. With a stable body and open resonating cavities behind the point of restriction, the semivowels can positively contribute to consistent resonance rather than impede it.

> *Trap:* It is common to hear nasal consonants sung with less than an Open Throat, either a lax throat or a tense throat. In both instances, although the consonant may be clear, full-throated resonance is missing. Behind the [m], both mouth and throat can and should retain much the same openness as for the [ɑ]. Although the [n] blocks the entrance to the mouth entirely, spaces behind that point of restriction should not be unduly constricted. The Open Body is important in allowing the throat to stay freely open even though the precise shape of the resonators changes with the consonant.

Non-nasal consonants that can sustain a pitch include the following: [l] [r] [v] [w] [z]. Even though vowels are the primary carriers of the vocal line, these consonants can contribute significantly to the vocal flow because of their capability to carry pitch. Although sustaining these consonants is not desirable, they are nonetheless valuable for the flow of a vocal line. Like all vowels and consonants, they should be made as forward as possible so as not to crimp the spaces behind them.

Some consonants are sheer noise. They should not be sustained and are not contributors to a *legato* line. However, they enunciate words, so they must be executed, clearly and quickly. They are often rather extreme in their restriction of air, so care needs to be taken not to allow them to tighten the vocal tract, except where closure is absolutely necessary and only for a brief moment. Despite these potential problems, these consonants can be very expressive.

The noise consonants are the following: [f] [h] [p] [s] [t] [k] [ks]. They have no capability for pitch or vocalized sound. They are mere noise. However, there is no reason why the throat cannot stay open and free behind the first five of them. The [k] and [ks] are not as kind to the Open Throat, as they require a complete blockage of air flow with the tongue touching the roof of the mouth. Access to both the mouth and the nose is blocked. The singer must execute them crisply but immediately return to an unrestricted throat position. Care should be taken that restrictions do not negatively affect preceding or subsequent vowels. While more energy is needed for these consonants for them to be heard, the singer must be careful that energy is not equated to unnecessary tension or pushing. The Open Body must not be compromised before, during, or after the consonant.

Some consonants momentarily stop the air flow but, unlike those listed in the aforementioned paragraph, include a vocalized sound, although a thwarted one. They include [b] [d] [g] (as in *got*) [dʒ] (as in *jump*). The stoppages for these consonants occur at different places: at the lips for [b], behind the upper teeth between the tongue and hard palate for [d], between the tongue and the back roof of the mouth for the [g], and toward the front between the tongue and the roof of the mouth for the [dʒ]. The thwarted vocalized sound is easily recognizable in the initial consonants of the first word in the following pairs: *ban* / *pan*, *dad* / *tad*, *got* / *cot*, *jump* / *chump*. The initial consonant in the second word of each pair is mere noise, without vocalized sound.

It is clear that consonants, more than vowels, have the unfortunate potential of impeding a free-flowing tone far beyond what is necessary for the consonants themselves. The singer must use only as much movement as necessary to achieve these consonants and then return to the more open position of throat and mouth immediately.

THE KINESTHETIC EXPERIENCE OF FORWARD ARTICULATION

The overview of vowels and consonants gives context to the exercises that follow. As indicated, the tongue, lips, jaw, and soft palate must establish independence of movement so that they don't negatively engage adjacent muscle groups. Forward Articulation should be the goal for all vowels and most consonants. As always, the Open Body and Open Throat must be intentional for the sake of resonance, while Forward Articulation must be deliberate for the sake of enunciation.

The following exercises are physical, both beginning and ending with proper posture, Open Body, and Open Throat as preconditions for success with the vocalizations. Without those kinesthetic preparations, the vocalizations have little value. The tone is a product of them, for good or bad. Too often singers focus on the tone as a starting point rather than on the kinesthetic experience that produces good tone. Aiming for the tone without first focusing on the body as the musical instrument puts the cart before the horse, so to speak. It is likely to encourage superficial manipulation rather than a well-integrated technique. Good tone and good articulation are products of a good musical instrument. The singer's body is that musical instrument.

The exercises are few in number and, on the surface, simple. The emphasis is on quality rather than quantity. Move slowly through them, integrating the steps in a concerted and mindful manner that focuses on the physicality of the musical instrument. Working in this way might seem tedious, but it is the most direct path to improvement.

Recently, a student came to her lesson having made some significant progress over the weekend on a particularly challenging issue that she had been struggling with. I commented that it was apparent that she had done some good learning since her last lesson. She said that she had discovered that going slower made things come faster—to my mind, a major insight! I urge you to go slowly through the following exercises, focusing on details that lead the singer toward a quality kinesthetic experience. The tone will reflect that quality.

The vocal problems of a singer dictate the steps that must be taken to overcome them. Although every singer is unique, there are some problems that are common to many singers. I considered that as I set the order and organization of the following exercises. While I think that these will be relevant to most, if not all, singers, they certainly won't apply to everyone equally. However, the Three Steps undergird all of them, and they *are* relevant for all singers.

Along with issues of poor posture and poor breathing, I have found that there are two primary areas that negatively affect the tonal product: a tense jaw with limited range of movement and insufficient pharyngeal space. These occur at all levels of singing, from beginning to advanced. The following exercises offer suggestions for directly addressing these issues in the context of an Open Body and Open Throat, without which the vocalizations will not be effective. As Forward Articulation is layered, its integration with the other two steps is crucial. The OOFing mantra should be helpful in maintaining focus.

The Dropped Jaw

Until the jaw is released, finding freedom in the articulators and throat is nearly impossible. A released jaw can be considered a precondition of free articulation. Therefore, it is addressed first. The dropped jaw is important for encouraging the Open Throat both for the beginner who has an undeveloped concept of tone and for the advanced singer who is engaging in some kind of "throat control" involving the jaw.

It is rare that tension exists in only one place. A tight jaw is most often only one link in a chain of tensions. Because of this, if one link in the chain can be broken, the others are often disempowered. The yawning breath with a dropped jaw is a deterrent to constricting tensions.

The deeply dropped jaw is not completely relaxed. However, it is needed when singing high and/or loud. At this point in the discussion, though, its purpose is to break the habit of constricting tensions and to encourage a wider range of movement in the jaw.

Although it is easiest to deeply drop the jaw on an open vowel such as [ɑ], it is helpful with many other vowels and consonants as well, particularly for singing high or with greater volume. For many singers, that probably means opening farther than is familiar or comfortable, but it should encourage more independence between articulators and resonating cavities.

The deeply dropped jaw is possible because of the flexibility of the joint between the jaw and skull. When the jaw is in an open, released position, a hollowed-out space in the joint can be felt in front of the ear. To feel this, place a finger at the top of the jaw just in front of the ear while opening the jaw. This kind of opening is needed for high or loud singing. In the middle or low range with a relatively soft dynamic level, the jaw opening can be lessened. However, the deeply dropped jaw is used in many of the following exercises for reasons given earlier.

I should caution here that some singers have a dysfunction of this joint, casually referred to as TMJ, a shortened form of "temporomandibular jaw dysfunction." The singer with this condition may not be physically able to release the jaw or may experience pronounced pain or jaw lock during the opening effort. In such cases, the singer should work with a doctor who specializes in TMJ.

If other singers resist dropping the jaw to the point of release, they might be helped by putting three to four fingers between the upper and lower front teeth while singing the five singer's vowels. Few singers like this exercise, but it disallows the constricting influence of a tense jaw and demands tongue action that is independent of the jaw. Without tension in the jaw or tongue, the singer is more likely to experience an Open Throat. This is not to say that opening of the throat must always be accompanied by a deeply dropped jaw but that the throat can remain fully open behind all vowels and most consonants, including those that require moderate air restriction of some kind.

EXERCISE

Beginning with a speaking voice that is served by the singer's Open Body and Open Throat, five vowels provide the vehicle for a sustained, resonant vocal line.

- Establish postural alignment as an active lift of the body through a spinal stretch.
- With a deeply dropped jaw, prepare the Open Body and Open Throat with an expansive breath. Maintain this for a second or two before beginning to phonate. Without disturbing the spaces of the Open Body or Open Throat, speak the vowels on a sustained tone.
- Inserting finger tips, if necessary, speak and sustain [a] [e] [i] [o] [u] on one continuous tone with five different colors, in a smooth unbroken line. Remember that because vowel sounds are unrestricted, none of the movements of articulation should impede the tonal flow. The five articulations should be done with tension-free movements of the tongue and lips, with the tip of the tongue remaining loosely forward even when the rest of the tongue may be lifting. The most difficult vowel with such a dropped jaw is the [i] because the lift of the tongue is high and facilitated by the front blade of the tongue. With a deeply dropped jaw, it may not be possible to get a completely clear vowel,

but for now, the purpose is to encourage independence between the tongue and the Open Throat. As more skill is obtained, the jaw will be able to relax its drop for an [i] without losing pharyngeal space.

EXERCISE

- After speaking the aforementioned vocalization, try it on a singing tone beginning with figure 5.1a.

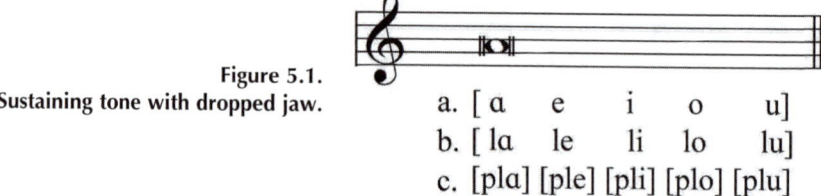

Figure 5.1.
Sustaining tone with dropped jaw.

a. [a   e   i   o   u]
b. [la   le   li   lo   lu]
c. [pla] [ple] [pli] [plo] [plu]

- With a deeply dropped jaw, prepare the Open Body and Open Throat with a singer's inhalation.
- Sing the vowels of figure 5.1a on a pitch in your comfortable middle range using the same guidelines given for the spoken vocalization regarding the fluidity of vowel changes and continuity of vocal line.
- Maintain the postural lift and expansive body and throat throughout the entire line of vowels.
- Take this vocalization up a few steps, but don't go beyond the middle range.

Although resonance per se has not yet been explicitly factored in, singing the vocalization with an Open Body and Open Throat should elicit a freer, richer tone than what you might expect. It is an important step in articulating with a *chiaroscuro* tonal palette.

An Enemy to Forward Articulation: A Tongue That Pulls Back

Before continuing to the vocalizations of figure 5.1b and 5.1c, the issue of an errant tongue needs to be addressed because it can jeopardize Forward Articulation as well as resonance itself. It is quite common for the tongue to pull back, particularly when the body is not doing its job. To compensate, the tongue becomes entwined with the throat in what I have earlier labeled "throat support." This leads to multiple tensions and technical faults, muddy vowels being one of them.

Rather than working with the tongue as a first line of defense, a final check of the body would be beneficial, as it might be the root of the tense tongue problem.

Only if this is fixed will the relaxation of the tongue be possible. Once the body is addressed, direct attention to the tongue will be more successful in eliminating any remaining tension.

EXERCISE

The consonant [l] is effective for loosening the tongue because of its pronounced movements. Quick and deliberate tongue movements that are loosely executed can be very helpful in relaxing extraneous tensions. Now refer back to the vocalization in figure 5.1b.

- Prepare the singer's body and pause a moment at the peak of inhalation before beginning to phonate.
- Start with a deeply dropped jaw and loose tongue. Sing [l ɑ] [l e] [l i] [l o] [l u] with a continuous flow of consistently resonating sound. Keep in mind that the [l] is one of those consonants that can carry pitched sound. It is helpful for making a consistent, uninterrupted vocal line. The tip of the tongue must lift up behind the upper front teeth and then flip forward and down with release. The [l] must be executed with a conscious effort to maintain the space behind the lifted tongue in both throat and body. The amount of movement required of the tongue for this consonant discourages tension, and speeding up the exercise helps even more.
- Take this vocalization up a few steps, always maintaining the stable, expanded body.

EXERCISE

Forward Articulation can also be encouraged by placing a [p] before each syllable as in figure 5.1c. Sing the following vocalization based on the guidelines given here:

- Once again, prepare the Open Body and Open Throat as described throughout part II. Take your yawning breath with a dropped jaw as if you are about to begin the vocalization with an [ɑ] rather than [plɑ]. Establishing the resonant space of the [ɑ] before placing the [p] in front of it will model the resonant space that should remain behind the lip closure of the [p].
- Sing [plɑ] [ple] [pli] [plo] [plu] as in figure 5.1c. Unlike the [m] or the [l], the [p] cannot sustain a pitch, and the tone is momentarily stopped; nevertheless, you should maintain the resonating space behind it. While the [p] requires "plosive action," be sure that the in-and-down muscles do

not put the body in a pushing mode. This consonant can be produced in the front of the mouth with a well-directed flow of breath while the body maintains its lift.

- Don't spread the mouth at any point, particularly on the [e] and [i]. The vertical framework for all vowels is aided with a dropped jaw, lowered larynx, and deep breath.
- Take this vocalization up and/or down by half steps, but stay in your middle range.

The Chiaroscuro *Balance*

It is completely possible and not uncommon to hear clear articulation with a tone that lacks full resonance. In many ways, this is similar to everyday speech as discussed earlier. In fact, when I hear this in the singing voice, I refer to it as speaking on pitch as opposed to singing on pitch. To have clear articulation with the resonance expected of fine singing, the focus must be on the Open Throat and Forward Articulation as a pair that are both independent and interdependent. If they work together, clear enunciation is possible in a fully resonating tone. To achieve the *chiaroscuro* balance, the dark/light polarities become partners in resonance via the Open Throat in back and Forward Articulation in front.

EXERCISE

My observation has been that it is more common for singers to favor the light quality over the dark quality in their tonal palette. I find this to be true at all levels of singing even though richness of tone is of primary importance for continuing development, even for lighter voices. However, some singers manipulate a dark quality resulting in various tensions, and this is also counterproductive to further development. All singers must seek out a tone that is balanced with both dark and light qualities, or they cannot function in the fullness of their vocal instrument.

Both of the following vocalizations encourage the *scuro* element, the dark quality in the tone, but without minimizing the *chiaro* element, the light quality. Vowels with a natural propensity for richness are used as models for brighter vowels that sometimes can become thin. The dark [o] is paired with its bright counterpart, the [e], and the [u] is similarly paired with [i]. Although each pair shows an obvious contrast between dark and bright, the two vowels of each pair share certain resonance properties associated with the dark element, a common thread of richness. The [o] [e] pair are explored in figure 5.2a in an effort to balance the *chiaroscuro* elements.

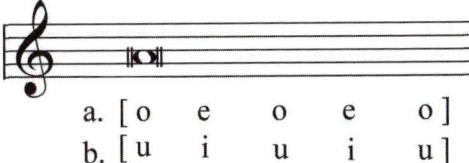

a. [o   e   o   e   o]
b. [u   i   u   i   u]

Figure 5.2. *Chiaroscuro* balancing.

- With the preparation of good posture and a loosely dropped jaw (slightly less than the deeply dropped jaw, because of the middle range pitch and closed vowels), prepare the Open Body and Open Throat. Check that the tongue lies loosely at the bottom of the mouth.
- For a few seconds, maintain the spaces created with the Open Body, dropped jaw, and yawning breath. This is an important step in raising your consciousness of the state of expansion and readiness for singing. When beginning to make sound, you must maintain this state rather than letting the body collapse, push, or lockset.
- With a sustained singing tone, begin the vocalization with the richest [o] possible, keeping in mind that the jaw should remain as dropped as possible while still accommodating the lip pursing. Intentionality of the Open Throat should not diminish when the lips are in this position.
- Stay focused on maintaining the body's expansion while singing. Continue the muscular efforts of inhalation even as you provide air flow for the tone. As long as the lifting of the body continues, you need not worry about breathiness.
- Move from the [o] to the [e] with as little change in the articulators as possible and keeping them as forward as possible. That noted, the tongue must move from a lift in the back of the mouth to a more forward lift, and the lips must release the pursing needed for the [o]. When moving to the [e], don't allow any diminishment of space in the pharynx or lift of the body.

Trap: Many singers unnecessarily spread the mouth for the [e]. This vowel needs no mouth, lip, or jaw movement. Like some other vowel sounds, the [e] is achieved solely with tongue movement and should not involve extraneous movements. The upper lip should reveal some of the upper teeth on the [e] and for all vowels except the [o] and [u], but this is usually the natural position of a relaxed mouth.

- The [e] should not lose any richness of the [o] but should only add brightness to the quality with the change of vowel template. It should be formed in a vertical framework rather than the horizontal framework of a spread mouth position. Thinking vertically is not just a bit of imagery but part of the physical framework of the vocal tract, including the mouth and jaw.
- Move this vocalization up by a few half steps, but stay in your middle range for now.

EXERCISE

Now sing the vocalization of figure 5.2b, employing the [u] and [i] instead of the [o] and [e]. The [u] is the darkest of all vowels and the [i] the brightest. Still, their common resonance properties allow the [i] to retain the richness of the [u] as well as additional brightness.

- With the preparation of good posture and loosely dropped jaw (slightly modified from the deeply dropped jaw), prepare the Open Body and Open Throat. Check that the tongue lies loosely at the bottom of the mouth.
- With a sustained singing tone, begin the vocalization with as much throat space behind the [u] as possible. The jaw should remain as dropped as possible while allowing the lip pursing. This should not diminish the Open Throat.
- Focus on maintaining the Open Body and Open Throat while singing.
- Move from the [u] to the [i] with as little change in the articulators as possible and formed as forward a possible. That noted, the tongue will move from a high lift in the back for the [u] to a high lift in the front for the [i], the latter of which requires the release of lip pursing.

Trap: As with the [e], be sure that the [i] is not accompanied by a spread mouth. The mouth need not be involved in this vowel. Although it is good to retain the richness of the [u], do not pull the upper lip down in a misplaced effort to artificially darken the [i]. This is extraneous and indicates tension that is sure to attract other tensions. It is important to remember that rich tones can be shaped with bright vowel templates such as the [i]. (Recall the cookie press analogy!) It would not be uncommon if, despite these cautions, you still find the [i] to be thin, white, or strained. If so, you need to pay greater attention to separating the tongue movement from the dropped jaw and/or the Open Throat. Another likely culprit could be a loss of lift in the body.

EXERCISE

The following exercise (figure 5.3) demonstrates the contrast between closed vowels and the [ɑ]. In a voice that is more or less naturally good, lack of training can most often be detected on the [ɑ]. It is easily susceptible to loss of clarity and ring. Compared to other vowels, the pitch span of its resonance properties are more limited, making it more difficult to incorporate both depth and ring in the tone. It is the most

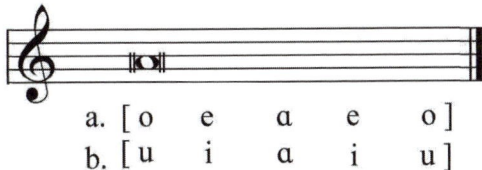

a. [o   e   a   e   o]
b. [u   i   a   i   u]

Figure 5.3.   Adding the [a].

open vowel, making it more vulnerable to losing air if the body is not doing its work. Compensatory measures such as pulling the tongue too far back would have a negative impact, as would forming the [a] in a horizontal rather than vertical framework. Insufficient breath management could be responsible for both of these issues.

To offset these challenges, the vocalization of figure 5.3 surrounds the [a] with either the [e] or [i]. These bright vowels, infused with the richness of the darker vowels preceding them, surround the [a] in an effort to guide it into resonant consistency and clarity. Forming all vowels in a vertical rather than horizontal framework contributes to a consistent *chiaroscuro* balance.

EXERCISE

- Prepare the Open Body and Open Throat in preparation for singing the vocalization in figure 5.3a.
- Follow the same guidelines for preparation and execution as given for the vocalizations in figure 5.2. Allow no spread of the mouth with either the [e] or [a].
- Manage the flow of breath easily and consistently with a lifted body using the natural richness of the [o] as a model for the [e] and the brightness of the [e] as a model for the [a].
- Make sure that the body does not collapse on [a], a vowel prone to spilling breath if not managed well. The verticality of the [a] should include the tall lift of the body.
- Since the [a] might tend to fall prey to swallowing muscles, pulled back tongue, or soft palate interference, give your attention to bringing the breath forward to the vowel template rather than letting the vowel get entwined in back. This is a basic principle of Forward Articulation.
- When you are comfortable that the [a] is maintaining the same clarity and richness as the other vowels, try to linger on it awhile.
- At this point, you might also try increasing the volume on the [a] and accommodating that effort with increased jaw drop and abdominal activity. Maintaining the body expansion, the opposite of squeezing, prevents pushing for volume even though more breath pressure is required.
- Take this vocalization up by half steps, but don't go beyond the middle range yet.

EXERCISE

- Refer to figure 5.3b, and follow the same guidelines given for the vocalization in figure 5.3a. This time capitalize on the natural richness of the [u], and allow it to influence the [i] and [ɑ]. Continue the efforts of inhalation, and take care not to spread the mouth on the [i] or [ɑ].
- When you are comfortable with the quality of the [ɑ], linger on it awhile.
- Next, experiment with more volume. As you increase volume, you will need to allow the jaw to drop more deeply (vertically), especially for the [ɑ].
- Move up and down the scale by half steps, but stay in the middle range for now.

EXERCISE

Coming full circle from the first exercises in which the basic five vowels were both spoken and sung with good posture, the Open Body, and the Open Throat, you may now be able to realize a more complete *chiaroscuro* balance than earlier. To get off to a good start, the vocalization in figure 5.4 begins with the syllable [m o] before morphing into the [ɑ]. Although a breath follows, the first measure should be used to set up the singer's body and the tone quality that will carry through the next two measures.

Conventional notation is used for this vocalization because of its more specific rhythmic values, but the uninterrupted flow of tone should nevertheless remain a primary goal.

[mo   ɑ]   [ɑ   e   i   o   u   ma]

Figure 5.4.   Integrating vowels and consonant.

- With good posture, prepare the Open Body and Open Throat with a yawning breath. Maintain this expansion for a second or two before beginning the vocalization of figure 5.4. When beginning to phonate, do not collapse, push, or lockset the body.
- Make sure the [m] is formed with lips that are loosely together, with no hint of pressing them together. Make sure the spaces behind the lips, the mouth and pharynx, remain fully and flexibly open.
- Morph into the rich [o] from a spacious [m] with gently pursed lips, only slightly modifying the drop of the jaw, but maintaining the Open Throat and

Open Body. The efforts of inhalation continue through the vocalization except for the rest in the first measure.

- In the first measure, when morphing to the [ɑ] template from the [m o], allow the added brightness to the tone without losing richness.
- The quarter rest at the end of the first measure should be used for relaxing the diaphragm and rib muscles for a brief moment but not the muscles of good posture. Good posture is a constant element. During rests as much as when singing, the chest should remain comfortably high, the thorax actively lifting up from the lower body.
- Then, even though the inhalation may be quicker than what you've practiced so far, use the dropped jaw to encourage full and flexible open spaces in preparation for the next measure.
- Begin the [ɑ] in the second measure with the same quality achieved in the first measure. Each vowel should morph into the next using only the movements of articulation needed for each vowel and no more.
- Form the vowels in a vertical framework including the tall lift of the body.

If the efforts of inhalation continue through the whole exercise, the articulators do their job without extraneous tensions, and the larynx remains dropped, the vowels should emerge clearly enunciated, efficient, and with a *chiaroscuro* balance in the tone.

EXERCISE

Once clarity of vowels is achieved with ease while singing a single sustained pitch in the middle range, the singer can proceed to singing scales. The tone in the descending scale should remain as consistent as possible through Forward Articulation of vowels and the maintenance of the Open Throat and Open Body.

The suggested starting pitch for figure 5.5 is raised slightly so that the female voice is not likely to enter chest voice territory on the lower pitches. If the male voice is singing this vocalization an octave below, he will likely be in the chest voice territory throughout. As always, you may alter the pitch level as you need to, but always stay in your middle range, not crossing any transition areas for now.

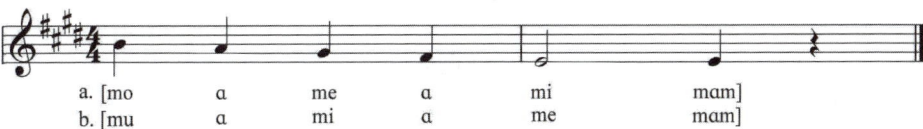

Figure 5.5.   Vowels on a scale.

- Follow the same guidelines given for figure 5.4 with regard to the preparation as well as the relationship between vowels and the [m].
- The [m] must be superimposed on the open spaces of the vowels, not restricting the tone in any way. Use the final [m] as a means of gently finishing the phrase in full resonance rather than allowing any diminishment of resonating space and tone quality. The tendency might be to relax the throat before the vocalization is finished.
- Focus on keeping the [i] and [e] full and vertical without any impingement on pharyngeal space.
- Other vowels can easily be substituted as in figure 5.5b.

There are countless scales and arpeggios that singers use in their training, but the intent here is not to be comprehensive. It is rather to provide foundational tools for confronting the most common challenges to vocal technique in the simplest way possible. Simple exercises done well are more productive than complicated ones done poorly. Integration of the Three Steps is no small matter. It is at the heart of beautiful singing and is the basis of finer skill development, as addressed in part III.

Simple or complex, no vocalise should simply warm up the voice, nor can it make a singer sing better. To be successful, a vocalise must be prepared by the whole body, as the kinesthetic process of fine singing requires. Beautiful tones are the product of a well-prepared vocal instrument.

SUMMARY

One of the essentials of beautiful singing is clear enunciation of the text. However, it is far more than that; it is a participator in resonance. Vowels and consonants lend countless colors to the vocal line and offer much potential for expressivity. Forward Articulation suggests that the formation of vowels and consonants takes place as forward as possible so as not to impede the resonance of the Open Throat and the flow of the breath. Movements of articulation should be free of undue tension or exaggerated efforts, and must not interfere with a smooth, flowing, consistent vocal line except where momentary constriction is required for a consonant. Forward Articulation, integrated with the Open Body and Open Throat, enables fine enunciation without impeding the *chiaroscuro* balance of light and dark elements of resonance. It should enhance and embellish resonance with great variety.

With the simplest exercises and vocalizations possible, the Three-Step Approach offers a mindful and methodical perspective on equipping the singer's body for enabling good breath management, resonance, and enunciation for all levels of singing. Now it is time to move on to higher levels of functioning and finer skill. Part III addresses issues of registration, developing the upper vocal range, and singing *legato*. The Three Steps, with OOFing mantra at hand, will continue to provide the foundation for these skills but with more finely tuned discernment. The exercises become somewhat more complex but only as necessary to convey the underlying principles of each skill. The refinements addressed continue to be presented in the context of kinesthetic experience, the experience of the applied art of singing.

Part III

REFINEMENTS TOWARD GREATER SKILL

· 6 ·

Principles of Registration

$\mathcal{T}$he Three-Step Approach as described in parts I and II is a concise way of focusing on the essentials of beautiful singing—fine breath management, resonance, and enunciation—in their most elemental forms. With the kinesthetic experience of the Open Body, Open Throat, and Forward Articulation, a vocal technique that leads to beautiful singing can begin to take form. Part III now explores the ways in which the voice can gain greater refinement and skill, particularly in the areas of registration, the upper vocal range, and *legato* singing.

Infused with additional subtlety, finesse, and adaptability, the Three Steps remain foundational to the refinements required of demanding vocal music. "What goes around comes around" is an adage that applies to the ubiquitous Three Steps and the multilayering that enables greater refinement. Addressing those refinements begins with this chapter on the principles of registration.

A vocal register is a pitch area in the vocal range with somewhat of a homogeneous sound quality that is distinguishable from the quality of another pitch area. The lower register tends to produce a heftier sound quality than the lighter quality produced in the upper register. While the lower quality might be associated with the male voice and the upper quality with the female voice, both can be accessed by men and women. Specific physiological functions, particularly in the larynx, give rise to the various registers.

Register adjustments might be considered to be gears of the vocal mechanism. The need to "shift gears," so to speak, is in some ways similar to manually shifting gears in a car or on a bicycle. The gear that is efficient when moving slowly is not efficient when moving faster. In the voice, the gear that works for low pitches is not efficient for high pitches. Efficiency minimizes the workload of singing, allowing ease and flexibility in the voice. Shifts that are executed skillfully are relatively imperceptible, but they enable a smooth, uninterrupted vocal line.

Registration adjustments cannot be directly controlled by the singer, but the physical processes that enable these adjustments can. The Three Steps focus on those physical processes as the ingredients of registration skill.

Registration function can understandably seem complex. Although there are many similarities between the female and male experience of registers, there are aspects that are unique to each of them, and this can complicate the discussion. For that reason, the female and male voice are addressed separately.

The numerous exercises in this chapter constitute a mere sampling of many useful ways of approaching registration issues. They were chosen because of their potential to "cut to the quick" of registration adjustment. With a continuing commitment to cultivated simplicity of thought and process, they were designed to clarify registration, in terms of both understanding and application. Guidelines for their execution stress the importance of the kinesthetic experience as the source of registration facility. The exercises are organized in groups, with each group focusing on a particular issue. Although they may appear to be simple, slow and mindful practice can offer significant insight leading to greater skill.

The exercises in part II are limited to the middle pitch range simply because good vocal technique can most easily be learned and executed in a pitch area where greater finesse is not needed. In this chapter, the pitch range slowly broadens but is not specifically moved into the upper range yet. That comes in the next chapter, and skills of registration are an important element of it.

THE CONTEXT

Much of the vocal repertoire for a trained singer requires at least a two-octave span. Such a span is suggested in figure 6.1 for each of five voice types. Keep in mind that voices are unique and that there are different types of voices within the five voice types. The spans vary accordingly. What remains constant is that any two-octave span of pitches likely involves more than one register.

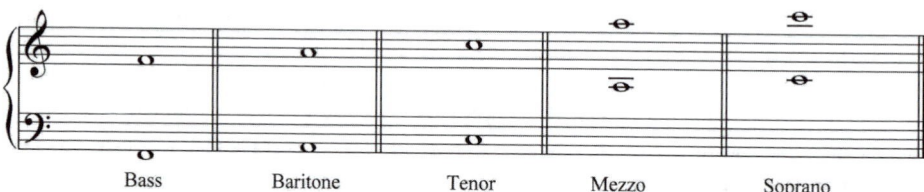

Bass   Baritone   Tenor   Mezzo   Soprano

Figure 6.1.   Repertoire range requirements.

There are many opinions about how many registers there are, but the two-register theory is particularly well supported physiologically. It consists of the heavy mechanism (for lower pitches) and the light mechanism (for higher pitches). "Mechanism" refers here to the actions of the vocal folds and related structures as addressed in chapter 4, on resonance. "Mechanism" and "register" are interchangeable. The size, shape, and tension of the vocal folds and the manner in which they vibrate reflect the register being used. When in the heavy register, the folds are shorter and thicker and vibrate slowly through the depth of the folds. When in the light register, the folds are stretched longer and thinner with the thin edge vibrating. At the extremes of the two registers, the sounds are significantly different.

You may be familiar with the terms "chest voice" and "head voice." These terms are another way of labeling the two primary registers, with "chest voice" being another name for the heavy mechanism or register and "head voice" being another name for light mechanism or register. These labels may wrongly give the impression that different registers resonate in different places. The reality is that all tones originate in the larynx and are resonated in the pharynx, mouth, or nose. A singer might feel a little buzz in the chest for low tones or a sensation in the head for high tones, but those sensations are not the source of resonance. However, they give rise to the term "chesty" for a low hefty sound and "heady" for a high light sound. Most people, trained singers or not, would get a relatively correct sense of the quality being described by these nontechnical terms.

The area of demarcation between chest voice and head voice might be called the primary transition. Exactly where it occurs in the singer's vocal range differs somewhat depending on the voice type, but it is usually within a step or two of Eb above middle C, the same pitch for both male and female voices. This means that the primary transition for a certain tenor might be the same pitch as for a certain soprano. This is quite remarkable given that female and male vocal ranges are an octave or so apart from each other. The reason for this is that the tracheas of males and females are similar enough in size to impart a similar element of resonance to both voices. Transitions tend to be slightly higher for lighter voices, such as tenors or sopranos, and slightly lower for darker voices, such as mezzos, baritones, and basses.

The pitches above the primary transition might be considered head voice territory, and the pitches below it might be considered chest voice territory. The register that is appropriate for low pitches is not appropriate for high pitches and vice versa. To achieve a consistent tone quality throughout the range, trained singers must learn to traverse these disparate sections of the voice as smoothly as possible.

Traversing the primary transition smoothly is experienced differently by the two genders. As the male goes upward through it, he moves toward his upper range. As the female goes upward through it, she does this near her lower range. This is a significant difference. Another difference is that the female has a second transition an octave above the primary transition. However, because it lies at the beginning of her upper range, the experience of singing in that area is similar to that of a male voice above the primary transition. Males and females alike require significantly more energy when singing in their upper ranges. This will be covered more thoroughly in the next chapter.

In figure 6.2, the upper pitch in each measure indicates the primary transition, and the lower pitch indicates the lower preparation for it a fourth below the primary transition. This area can be larger or smaller depending on the volume and vowel and may move slightly up or down depending on the voice type and what effect is sought for a particular pitch.

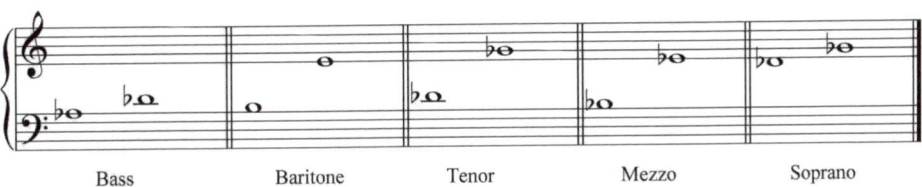

| Bass | Baritone | Tenor | Mezzo | Soprano |

Figure 6.2. Primary transitions and preparatory areas.

Registration adjustments are not limited to two choices, either chest voice or head voice. They must be made incrementally on a series of pitches leading up to and away from the primary transition. To negotiate the whole vocal range with an even vocal line from the bottom to the top requires gradations of registration adjustments that allow blends of chest voice and head voice. Such blends are useful below or above the primary transition.

Because a consistent vocal line requires many register adjustments throughout the vocal range, as opposed to a single adjustment at the primary transition, a two-register theory comes up short. This is where multiregister theories come in. At the very least, some sort of middle ground needs to be accessed, or the smooth line from the bottom to the top of the range is impossible.

The blending of chest and head voice has aptly been called the "middle voice," an area where the folds do not function solely in chest voice or head voice but rather in combinations of both in varying proportions. A lighter sound reflects a higher percentage of head voice in the tone, and a heftier sound reflects a higher percentage of chest voice in the tone. There is infinite variety in blends.

Not to be confused with the middle of the vocal range, the term "middle voice" as used here refers to a registration phenomenon, the blend between chest and head. For instance, the male preparatory "middle voice" blend is near or into his upper range, substantially higher than the middle of his vocal range.

Even though the middle voice is technically a blend rather than a separate register, it is sometimes referred to as a third register between chest voice and head voice. No matter how it is labeled, it is a bridge between chest and head that must be developed and balanced to maintain an even tone throughout the vocal range.

The vocal range then is a continuum of pitches from low to high. For the whole range to have consistent tone quality, pitches must morph seamlessly into neighboring pitches through skillful registration adjustments, the mechanics of which should not be apparent to the listener. Registration shifts minimize the workload, giving the singer an ease that is one of the prerequisites of beautiful singing. The shifts are enabled by the integration of the Open Body, Open Throat, and Forward Articulation, the specifics of which are emphasized and applied to the exercises that follow.

The chest–head proportions of a blend can fluctuate on a single pitch with volume changes. As the pitch grows louder, more chest quality enters, and as it grows softer, more head quality enters. However, the listener hears only a gradual *crescendo* or *decrescendo*.

The capacity of the vocal folds to function in chest and head voice modes and the blends reflect the flexible nature of the vocal folds themselves. Men speak primarily in the chest register but employ head voice or some blend to sing in their upper range. Women often, but not always, speak in their chest register but primarily sing in head voice or some blend. Both voices need both registers to function in the fullness of their instruments. Failing to access any part of the instrument is to sing with only a portion of the voice. It would be like weight training on one side of your body but not the other or learning to play the piano with the left hand but not the right hand. The chest quality gives warmth, depth, and richness to the voice, and the head quality gives brightness, flexibility, and ring to it. Chest–head blends enable an even vocal line in the continuum from low to medium and high pitches.

Despite the octave difference between male and female voices, there is much common ground with regard to registration issues. From low to high pitches, all voices must move with ease from a predominance of chest voice, to a flexible blend of chest and head, and, ultimately, to a predominance of head voice in the upper range. The voices differ only in where the adjustments occur relative to the span of their ranges. The middle range of the male voice naturally has more chest voice in it because it lies below the primary transition in chest voice territory. The middle range of the female voice has more head voice in it because it lies above the primary transition in head voice territory.

Beyond the five voice types included in figures 6.1 and 6.2, some higher sopranos might have an upper extension, sometimes called the "flute voice." Some lower male voices might have a lower extension below the full chest voice, sometimes called "vocal fry." These extensions are not the focus here or in chapter 7. However, the principles of the kinesthetic experience of registration apply to these outer realms of range with only slight modifications.

Before continuing, it might be good to issue a word of caution about chest voice. Just because it has a heftier quality than head voice does not mean that it has a raw or forced quality to it, in either the male voice or the female voice. This apprehension could be the reason why some female singers are told to avoid it. While chest voice is capable of strength and volume, it must also possess warmth and flexibility. Appropriate registration can accommodate both.

In contemporary popular singing, male and female singers alike often sing chest voice far above the primary transition. Taking the chest voice excessively high for the sake of volume without any head voice blend usually prevents the proper development of a sturdy middle voice. When the chest voice can go no further in this manner, a weak version of head voice might be all that is available, resulting in an awkward "break" in the voice. Although there are pedagogues who teach relatively healthy ways of this style called "belting," it is not an appropriate technical model for classical singing and will not be addressed here.

At the other extreme is the female singer who has never ventured into the chest voice at all. She might have a weak middle voice for lack of a chest voice element. Without any chest voice in a descending melodic line, the volume must diminish even if the music and text imply emphasis and volume. However, delving into chest voice can be intimidating for such a singer, and she might need some assertiveness training to get it going! Ultimately, the chest voice should sound just as mellifluous as any other part of the vocal range, although that probably will not happen at first try.

The discovery of chest voice for the female is comparable to the discovery of head voice for the male. Since the male speaks and sings primarily in chest voice, the head voice might be completely new territory to him or totally absent. In such a case, higher pitches are met with struggle, and the middle range may lack warmth and flexibility. If the chest voice is not as strong as it should be, it could profit from much the same technical work as that of the female who needs to develop a stronger chest voice.

Having outlined some of the general principles of registration, the following exercises are designed to demonstrate various means of accessing or strengthening head, chest, or a blend in both male and female voices. As in previous chapters, the exercises are chosen and ordered based on my experience with singers and what their most common needs are. They may not apply to everyone.

The first two sections focus on the chest voice and are primarily for women. The next three sections focus on the head voice and are primarily for men. Many exercises are applicable to both voices. The section on volume-dictated adjustments is gender free.

As in earlier chapters, exercises combine two elements: guided physical preparations and the "vocalizations" that put the preparations to the test. The exercises in this chapter help to facilitate the complete kinesthetic experience required of singing with registration facility. As in earlier chapters, most vocalizations are shorter and simpler than typical "vocalises," but to sing them well demands an Open Body, Open Throat, and Forward Articulation. Consequently, the OOFing mantra is ever present.

CHEST REGISTER IN THE FEMALE VOICE

The chest voice is often the most underdeveloped segment of a female voice. This might be considered inconsequential since it is the least employed pitch area in the repertoire for most female singers. However, the lack of chest voice development negatively affects other segments of the voice, particularly in the middle voice, where a blend is necessary for full resonance.

The vocalizations in figures 6.3–6.8 and the accompanying guidelines are primarily for light voices that have accessed little, if any, chest voice.

Accessing and Isolating the Chest Voice

Exercises to encourage the chest voice begin below the primary transition but not so low that it is uncomfortable. Although the primary transition is close to the E♭ above middle C, it may vary slightly, either higher or lower. The pitch given in figure 6.3 should be receptive to chest voice in most voices, even if it is not strong. If you heed the OOFing mantra, the tone should strengthen quickly.

Vowels affect how and when chest voice is accessed. For example, the open [ɑ] is more accepting of chest voice than closed vowels such as [o] [u] [e] or [i]. Therefore, the exercises begin with [ɑ]. This vowel is useful for awakening an unused chest voice, correcting its use, or strengthening it. If you maintain and increase your body expansion as you move up the scale, you will not be tempted to push, and it will be safe to exercise the chest voice with vigor.

EXERCISE

If you are able, you may take the vocalization in figure 6.3 one or two steps beyond your primary transition even though that may be higher than what you will need in your songs or arias. Doing so will give you a margin of comfort above your highest usable chest tone.

So that you don't break out of chest voice before you reach the primary transition, you may need to increase the volume as you ascend the scale and drop your

Figure 6.3. Chest voice on [ɑ].

jaw more. With this exercise, you are training your vocal folds to remain in their relatively thick position rather than abruptly defaulting into the thinner vocal folds related to head voice. This exercise is not yet meant to bridge the transition between chest and head but simply to bolster the chest voice while ensuring that the breath is being managed well.

- Choose a pitch as low as you can comfortably phonate, approximately a fourth or fifth below the primary transition, close to the starting pitch of figure 6.3.
- Prepare the singer's body and throat as detailed in parts I and II. Take a yawning breath, always closer to a preyawn than a full yawn. Comfortably but intentionally maintain the expansion as you start singing. Sing assertively with substantial volume to encourage the heftier sound of chest voice, but do not allow the in-and-down muscles to create the push mode. You can sing as assertively and loudly as you want as long as you maintain the out-and-up efforts of body expansion.
- Take the vocalization up the scale by half steps until you reach the upper part of the chest register, either at the primary transition or just above it.
- Although the upper part of the female chest register is approximately an octave lower than the female's upper range, singing in the upper range of *any* register requires more energy than in the middle of it. The higher or louder the pitch, the more out-and-up energy and jaw drop will be needed.
- Increase the volume as you ascend. Make sure you are forming [ɑ] in a vertical rather than horizontal framework with an ample jaw drop and with no spread of the mouth position. You might feel the need for more abdominal assistance in energizing the breath pressure for assertive singing but not at the expense of rib cage expansion.
- If the sound is not strong, try opening the mouth farther, and be more assertive in creating more volume. Volume in the chest register is one of the benefits of using it. Head register cannot provide that in the lower range.
- If you are able to take chest voice to the E or F, do so. It will eventually make the E♭ easier if and when you need it to be in chest voice. However, don't feel obligated to go that high for now.

EXERCISE

To train muscles for the new experience of making strong chest tones, I often suggest what I call "noodling." This simply means hovering around a note or two where success has been achieved to nudge neighboring pitches into similar strength. In

Figure 6.4.   "Noodling" in chest voice.

the exercise in figure 6.4, when you find a pitch that is comfortably strong in chest voice, try to "noodle" around it, as in figure 6.4.

Noodling in chest voice in this way exercises your body and vocal folds for strength and endurance in this register. If it is easier for you and produces better results, you could noodle in half steps instead of whole steps.

- Prepare the Open Body and Open Throat with a loose and well-dropped jaw.
- Choose the lowest comfortably strong pitch in chest voice, much as you did for figure 6.3, and begin the vocalization of figure 6.4 on that pitch at a comfortably loud volume, always maintaining the lift of the body.
- Noodle around that starting pitch, in either whole or half steps, maintaining clarity, strength, and freedom. You may extend the noodling as long as your breath will allow without allowing the tone to weaken.
- Move the vocalization up by half steps. As you do so, especially if you're nearing the primary transition, you will need to increase your efforts of expansion and volume and drop your jaw more deeply. In time, your comfort zone should enlarge, and higher pitches will be able to retain a strong chest voice quality without undue tensions. Although singing in the upper end of any register requires more energy and assertiveness, there must be no push (as in body squeeze). Maintaining expansion puts a workload on the body but keeps the voice free.
- Once you've noodled in a comfortable area, take this exercise just past the transition if you can. (If you can't do that the first time you try, that's alright. You simply keep "asking" the folds to behave like chest voice folds. By giving them the space and volume that is needed, they will in time accommodate.)
- Keep [ɑ] in a vertical framework with a dropped jaw and no mouth spread.

EXERCISE

While [ɑ] is the most accommodating vowel for chest voice, singers must develop facility with chest voice on other vowels too. Although there are similarities of experience and sound among all five vowels in chest voice, there are differences as to where they are receptive to chest voice. This was discussed more thoroughly in chapter 4 on resonance. The singer needs to feel comfortable negotiating those differences.

Notating only one note for all five vowels when possible continues to be indicative of a single sustained tone with five different colors or timbres superimposed on it. Each vowel should morph seamlessly into the other without any drastic change of tone quality. Move slowly. Keeping a strict rhythm is not necessary. You may linger as long as you wish on any of the vowels for purposes of consciousness raising. Throughout this book mindful practice is recommended, and consciousness raising is integral to that.

Figure 6.5.   Chest voice and five vowels.

- Choose a comfortable pitch approximately a fourth or fifth below the primary transition, close to the one chosen for figure 6.4. Starting with the [ɑ], sing the five vowels on a single pitch in moderate to loud chest voice. The strength of the [ɑ] should act as a model for the other vowels. On the pitches suggested in figure 6.5, you should be able to stay in chest voice through all of the vowels, and they should retain a similar core, fullness, and freedom. Keep the vowel formations relegated largely to the tongue in as forward a position as possible so that it does not interfere with pharyngeal space. The jaw drop should be matched to the volume you are using: the louder the volume, the more deeply the jaw must drop.
- As you sing, maintain a stable body in a lifted position with muscles of inhalation always active.
- Sing one continuous tone with the five vowels superimposed on it by fluid movements of the tongue as well as lips for the [o] and [u].

The goal here is to encourage a strong chest voice, so sing it fairly loud but without push, a misplaced attempt at volume. The body and throat should be expansive, and the vowel formation should be vertical, assisted by a dropped jaw. The muscular efforts that maintain expansion will need to increase as you sing higher or with more volume. You should sing assertively and loudly without releasing the efforts of expansion.

- Move the vocalization up by half steps. To keep the [e] [i] [o] and [u] in chest voice further up the scale than what they may be so inclined, open the vowel formation a bit toward the vowels in the words *bet, bit, ought,* and *foot,* respectively. However, do this only as needed to maintain chest voice without losing vowel identity. Modification may be slight and is accomplished largely with increased jaw drop. On a vowel that is otherwise not receptive to chest voice in an area where dramatic emphasis is needed, this slight modification can create the access.
- As you near the higher part of the chest voice area, understand that the [e] [i] [o] and [u] may rightfully merge into head voice despite your efforts to take them higher. This is to be expected, but try to make the entrance into head register as full and smooth as possible. As with any transition area,

sometimes called a "lift area," giving an extra lift to the body should help facilitate a graceful transition. When the pitch gets beyond the transition into the middle voice, the jaw drop will be able to relax a bit since this area is the lower part of the head voice, not the upper part of chest voice.

- You might want to modify the vocalization of figure 6.5 by contrasting only one vowel at a time with the [ɑ], such as [ɑ o ɑ o ɑ] and [ɑ i ɑ i ɑ]. The same guidelines apply, and you might gain greater clarity about the behavior of the various vowels as they relate to chest voice.

Relationships between the Female Chest, Middle, and Head Voice

Up to this point, the goal for chest voice has simply been to encourage the full functioning of the heavy mechanism, especially for those women who have never fully exercised that part of their vocal instrument. For male and female singers, maintaining the lift of the Open Body while singing in the chest register eliminates the tendency to push the voice and encourages greater flexibility there. This may be the most significant missing element in an improperly produced chest voice.

Once a vigorous chest voice is established, its relationship to head voice can be explored. The following three vocalizations employ octave jumps to do this. Although the octave jump is not a magic bullet for balancing and developing the registers, it does have significant value. The octave jump can reveal a common denominator between a vigorous lower pitch in chest voice and the pitch an octave above in head voice. Jumping an octave puts the two pitches in direct contact with each other rather than moving between them in stepwise motion. Stepwise ascent requires gradual and fine registration adjustments and may exacerbate the singer's natural tendency to push a register higher than it should go. The element of surprise in the octave jump avoids those pitfalls.

EXERCISE

Once a vigorous chest voice exists, the singer should try to mirror it with an equally strong upper pitch in head voice. Because volume is a factor in these exercises, the jaw should drop deeply for them. Both pitches must be sung with a stable vocal mechanism grounded in the principles of Open Body, Open Throat, and Forward Articulation.

Because of the change of pitch in this vocalization, it must be notated with separate notes on the staff in figure 6.6. However, treating the three pitches as one continuous tone helps to ward off a "break" into a weak head voice.

Maintaining vigor and volume on the upper pitch is different from "carrying weight up," an expression that is more relevant to pushing a register up beyond where it should go. Pushing up a register does not allow the vocal folds to adjust properly. To enable the vocal folds to adjust to the size and shape required by head voice, the body has to anticipate the jump with an energized lift of the body and continue that lift while singing the upper note. This discourages pushing and encourages the appropriate register adjustments.

I warn you that octave jumps may not sound pretty at first and might make you think of yodeling! But the object is to "fool" the upper pitch into responding with the same vigor and core as in the developed chest voice. This is one of those vocalizations that can take the voice to a dramatically new place of resonance and create a strengthened blend area. Once it is established, it will serve as both a model and a pathway to a strong upper range.

At this point, I must admit that despite my lukewarm view of imagery as the primary means of teaching singing, I do use a bit of it when teaching the physical connection between the efforts of inhalation and the execution of large jumps. I had a teacher years ago who used the expression "drink in the air." The term seemed to suggest singing while inhaling, and that didn't really make sense to me at the time. Of course, the term is not meant to be literal. However, the muscular effort needed for inhalation is indeed much the same muscular effort needed to manage the breath. It counteracts collapse, push, or lockset in many situations but especially so in singing skips. Maintaining the body's expansion with a lift of the body helps to keep the larynx low and assists with the proper register adjustment, all the while enabling a smooth connection between two disparate pitches.

These vocalizations should be practiced for only short periods until you are sure that the body is the main source of energy, particularly with the out-and-up muscle action of inhalation and maintained expansion.

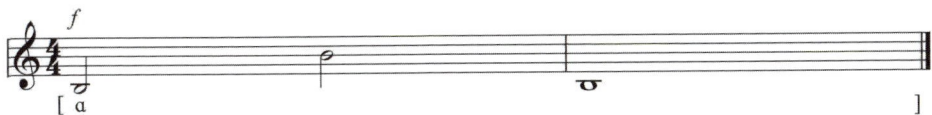

Figure 6.6.   Octave jumps.

Trap: There are two common mistakes made when doing octave jumps. One of them is to put an aspirated [h] before the vowel on the top note. This is indicative of pushing and blowing and commonly accompanies skips. Maintaining and even increasing the muscular efforts of inhalation as you make the octave jump disallows the interruption of an aspirated [h] and replaces it with a smooth connection between the lower note and the octave above. (Chapter 8 addresses the issue of *legato* more completely.) The other common mistake is to slide up to the top pitch. Move between the pitches cleanly without involving intermediate pitches.

- For the vocalization indicated in figure 6.6, choose a starting pitch close to the one you chose for figure 6.5, possibly a step higher. After preparing the Open Body and Open Throat (with some consciousness raising before continuing), drop the jaw in preparation for singing a vertical, vigorous, and comfortably loud [ɑ].
- Once the lower note is well established, plunge into the octave above with boldness but with a steady increase of body expansion and greater jaw drop. Be sure to lift the body as you move to the upper note to avoid any inward squeeze and resultant push. (This might feel more like taking air in than expelling it.) Even though the upper pitch may still be in the middle range, it will need extra space in body and jaw drop to accommodate the volume.
- If you tend to be resistant to a deeply dropped jaw, this would be a good time to insert three fingers between the front teeth.
- For the singer with an undeveloped chest–head blend, the upper pitch in the middle of the range might be much weaker than the one in chest voice. The goal is to have them match as closely as possible. This develops in time. Try different starting pitches, looking for one that might give more rewarding upper pitches. The more stable you can keep your body and the more connected the two pitches are, the more successful you will be.
- Sing all pitches assertively with as much volume as is comfortable without losing the Open Body. Since this will probably be quite loud, your jaw drop should be considerable for both pitches.
- Move the vocalization up the scale by half steps, going as high as is comfortable. You will probably reach a point where the upper pitches are stronger, probably near the secondary transition. This is to be expected. Take this vocalization one or two steps further up the scale, beyond the secondary transition, just barely into the upper range. Don't go further than that yet.
- When you hear a strong resonant tone at the upper octave, try noodling around it as suggested in figure 6.4. This should reinforce a fully grounded tone, develop muscle memory, and build endurance.

EXERCISE

Choose a pitch that can facilitate a strong lower and upper octave and will allow you to finish the vocalization just above the primary transition.

Figure 6.7.   Strengthening the middle voice.

- After preparing the Open Body and Open Throat and beginning a vigorous chest tone on the starting pitch, give the body an extra lift of the expanded body and morph into the upper octave. Although the rhythms suggested are purposeful, they are not mandatory. If you need more time on one or more of the notes to better observe what is happening on them, take the time.
- Sustain the upper pitch long enough to let it settle in before taking it down the five-tone scale. Maintain the strength and energy of the upper tone in all of the descending tones. Ordinarily the body energy can lessen somewhat in a descending scale, but since the focus here is on building volume and strength, efforts to maintain the energized expansion are important.
- Move the starting pitch down by half steps. As the final note nears the primary transition, you must be ready to accept chest voice, both mentally and physically. You must anticipate more jaw drop and energized expansion because you are entering the upper end of a register. The workload for this is managed by the expanded body. Don't be discouraged if your entrance into chest voice is not as graceful as you would like at first.
- As you continue down the scale, more and more tones will need to cross the transition. Expect that and prepare for it. With assertiveness take the vocalization down the scale as far as is comfortable, being sure to lift across the transition rather than push/squeeze into chest voice.
- Now repeat the same vocalization, but move the starting pitch up by half steps until the upper pitch crosses the secondary transition but only by a step or two.
- Before going on to the next exercise, go back to the earlier octave jumps of figure 6.6 to see if you can maintain the core in those upper notes better than you did in the first go around. Assuming that certain pitches have been coaxed into full strength, you might now be able to coax other pitches into similar strength. This is not just mental but physical as well. You are training very malleable muscles.

EXERCISE

Crossing the primary transition with grace and strength on any vowel is a needed skill for maintaining an even vocal line throughout the range. The following vocalization utilizes the five basic vowels.

Figure 6.8.　Melodic middle voice.

- Choose the same starting pitch that worked well for you in figure 6.7, one that allows the last note to occur just above the primary transition.
- Sing the octave jump, mirroring the vigor of the lower pitch with the higher pitch. Descend the scale on the [ɑ], and on the lowest pitch add the other vowels as notated. Try to maintain the richness, heft, and volume of the top note all the way down and through the other vowels. Look for chest voice as you near the bottom pitch rather than shying away from it. Opening the jaw and maintaining volume enhances your receptivity to chest voice. You may have to go down another step or two to access chest voice.
- Take the vocalization down by half steps noting the different functions of the vowels on various pitches. The [ɑ] will be the first to access chest voice, followed by the [o] and [e] and then the [u] and [i]. To encourage chest voice on the latter four vowels, maintain the volume and drop the jaw more. This opens the vowels so that they become more receptive.
- Be sure that all vowels are formed distinctly as far forward as possible with a loose tongue and lips. The jaw opening should relate to the volume: more drop for louder tones, less for softer tones, and always more drop for higher tones. At all times, the Open Body and Open Throat must be maintained.
- Any force or push will make the vocal mechanism too rigid to adjust. Once you cross the upper end of the chest voice and are more comfortable in the middle voice, the intensity of your outward expansion may relax a little.
- To encourage a seamless crossover, it will help to sing in a *legato* manner, even sliding a bit from one pitch to the next if needed. (This will not always be necessary.)
- Once you are secure with the descent, take the vocalization up the scale by half steps until the upper pitch goes one step beyond the secondary transition. Remember that when maintaining greater volume, especially toward the upper range, the jaw needs to be more open than in softer and lower singing. This naturally modifies vowels.

Up to this point, the emphasis has been on developing and strengthening the chest voice as a separate register and as a contributor to a full chest–head blend. For softer, subtle effects, the chest voice must be tamed with an infusion of flexible head voice.

EXERCISE

For musical situations that require delicacy and subtlety, the balance between chest and head voice must be tipped toward a lighter mechanism, even when in chest voice territory. This skill is probably lacking in singers who have been carrying the chest voice above the primary transition or forcing the voice in the chest register.

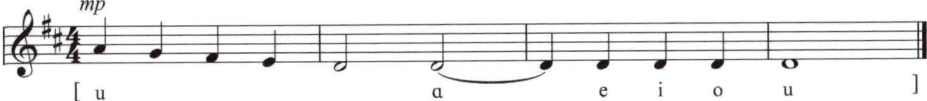

Figure 6.9.   Taming the chest voice (female version).

- Prepare the singer's body and throat.
- Begin softly with the [u] approximately a fourth above your primary transition. Its natural richness and receptivity to head voice sung at a soft dynamic level should discourage a heavy landing on the lower pitch near chest voice territory. It should model a delicate warmth and richness for the [ɑ] and subsequent vowels. Soft singing requires the Open Body and Open Throat of loud singing, not a smaller, less expansive instrument. However, the lift of the body might require slightly less effort unless in the upper range. The jaw drop in this range need not be deep.
- Take the vocalization down by half steps, maintaining a heady quality, until the bottom pitches are approximately a fourth lower than the primary transition.

EXERCISE

Next, sing the vocalization with the noodling tag notated in figure 6.10. When you reach the heady [ɑ], do not allow chest to take over. Although the first utterance of the [ɑ] on the second half of the beat in the second measure is the highest pitch, it should not be accented. Keep it in a light mechanism and in a smooth unbroken line.

Figure 6.10.   "Noodling" in light mechanism (female version).

- Follow the guidelines for figure 6.9, maintaining a consistent, light-flowing tone served by an Open Body and Open Throat. Compared to the louder and higher singing in some of the earlier exercises, this vocalization can be done with a slightly more relaxed expansion (but not collapsed). The jaw must remain loose although not deeply dropped.
- Make sure that you do not accent your first entrance into the [ɑ]. It is on the weak part of the beat and should act as a smooth connection to the rest of the notes, not a point of emphasis. Singers often tend to emphasize the higher notes in a phrase whether or not that is appropriate for the phrase or text. (More on this in the chapter on *legato*.)

- Only after you're able to maintain the heady quality, repeat the vocalization several times, each time increasing the volume. As you do that, chest voice enters the tone, and you will need to drop your jaw more as well as increase the efforts of expansion. You have choices as to how much chest or head voice you want in a given musical situation.

HEAD REGISTER IN THE MALE VOICE

In my experience, the head voice is the most misunderstood and flawed segment of the male voice. In young male singers, access to it may be completely lacking. In more advanced singers, it may lack freedom. Since males seldom speak in their head voices, with the possible exception of some light tenors, it is understandable that they are less familiar with head voice. So finding this register might seem like finding a new voice.

All male singers must access head voice to have a comfortable upper range, and to be beautiful, it must be free and flexible. This demands considerably more refinement than merely reaching those pitches. Even the pitch area just below the upper range, very common in repertoire, must have the benefit of chest–head blends for the sake of full and free resonance. Sometimes singers proceed as if pushing a little harder in the chest voice register will open the door to the upper range. This simply is not supported by physiology. Male singers need to discover a different gear and develop skill in its use.

When a male singer forces chest voice up, he creates more and more tension in the throat, and this gives the tone a strained quality. He will either have to continue the push to sing high or break into falsetto at some point. Unfortunately, head voice is sometimes called *falsetto*, and this is misleading. In this discussion, *falsetto* refers to a heady but weak sound that lacks intensity, volume, and clarity. It is not a fully grounded tone served by good breath management. Neither a pushed-up chest voice nor a lax *falsetto* is an acceptable option for the upper range in solo singing.

Adequate preparation for a smooth transition consists of gradual register changes in several pitches leading up to the transition, the preparatory areas indicated in figure 6.2. They must be facilitated with increasing energy of expansion as the pitch rises so that the vocal folds gradually assume the thinner, longer shape needed for head voice. Any push causes the folds to bulk up and resist the air, making head voice inaccessible. Greater jaw drop is also needed. Traversing the primary transition smoothly can be enabled only by the Open Body, Open Throat, and Forward Articulation. For both the male and the female, the energy needed for these three steps must significantly increase when nearing the transition into the upper range.

Because of the direct relationship between register adjustments and the Three Steps, the OOFing mantra continues to be emphasized in the exercises that follow. Vowels assist in accessing head voice. Since the [u] and [o] are more receptive to head voice than the [ɑ], they are used as models for the [ɑ] in the subsequent section.

Accessing Head Voice

Although specific register shifts are unique to each voice and fluctuate depending on the musical situation, the preparatory areas suggested in figure 6.2 are universal enough to be worthy of the singer's vigilance. Since the singer often cannot hear oneself correctly, judgments about when shifts are needed should be based on the ease of execution as much as on the pitch. The singer must develop kinesthetic awareness of tension anywhere in the vocal instrument, even when that tension is not glaring.

At the first moment that a voice has any tension in it while ascending, head voice has probably been avoided when it should have been incorporated. Thwarting the head voice at an early pitch might not adversely affect the tone in any obvious way at first, but it will hamper the pitches above, increasingly so with each step up. Waiting until one experiences obvious strain is too late.

EXERCISE

Access to the head voice is prepared by the pitches that begin approximately a fourth or fifth below the primary transition of E♭ or at the first appearance of slight strain. Most singers, especially those singers who have been pushing chest voice up, are surprised to find out how low in the range shift preparations might need to begin. Because many male singers can sing in that pitch area with no obvious strain, they normally associate those pitches with chest voice only and don't consider incorporating any head voice.

The following exercises should help the singer to locate his or her transition area under various circumstances. This requires kinesthetic discernment and is a more meaningful assessment than generalizations. The transition area is dynamic rather than static, fluctuating with the vowel and volume as much as pitch.

The following vocalizations are shown in bass clef, but they are not limited to use by baritones and basses. The pitches on the staves in figure 6.11 should serve all male voices well, including tenors, as some of the preparatory pitches are common to all voice types. They encourage the upper range by slightly decreasing the volume at the top (for now) and blending in more head voice with the help of the [o] and [u]. These vowels, coupled with more energy of expansion, enable a graceful crossing of the primary transition.

Trap: Be sure not to confuse "darker color" with a muddied vowel, a swallowed sound, a tongue pulled back, a clutching soft palate, or some other manipulation that interferes with Forward Articulation. However, compared to a pushed-up and spread chest voice, the true head voice has, indeed, a richer color because the increased body expansion helps the larynx stay low, resulting in rich resonance, the dark element of the *chiaroscuro* balance.

The rich color that is associated with the male head voice is sometimes referred to as "cover." Although I don't object to this term, it does sometimes conjure negative reactions, so it is not one of the staples of the Three-Step terminology.

As indicated in figure 6.11, the vocalization should be sung several times using a different vowel or combination of vowels each time. The ascending pitches in the first measure must incorporate more head voice in small increments with each step up. This is accomplished by closing the vowel in ascent while increasing the efforts of expansion particularly at the point of crossing the primary transition. This is an extremely important step in accessing head voice for the upper range. It is the opposite of pushing. No matter where a particular voice prepares for the transition or where the actual transition is, the kinesthetic experience is similar for all male voices.

Figure 6.11.   Encouraging the head voice.

Although the incorporation of head voice in ascent is assisted by closed vowels at the top, take care that this does not equate to any closure of pharyngeal space or diminishment of body expansion. The guidelines of figure 6.11 address the vocalizations in groups because of the similarities between the first three and last two.

- Prepare the Open Body and Open Throat for figure 6.11a–c with a yawning breath, taking care not to lose that spaciousness when the lips must purse for the [o] and [u]. At the onset of tone, the moment when the tone begins, be sure to maintain a stable expansion. Begin at a moderate volume level, and make a slight *decrescendo* on the first four notes so that you approach the top note gently rather than loudly. Sing this as one continuous tone.
- While increasing the efforts of expansion with each rise in pitch, especially as you approach the top note, morph into the [u] [i] or [e] on the fourth pitch without any accentuation of it. As always, the word "morph" is meant to suggest a gentle glide into the new vowel sound rather than an abrupt change. The tone should flow evenly from the bottom note through the top note and down again, even though you will be making registration adjustments to accomplish that.
- Move the vocalization up by half steps until you just cross over your primary transition wherever that is. The more you focus on the preparation and expansion, the more naturally the tones will cross over the transition. If you notice any tension on the way up, you are probably not lifting the body enough, singing softly enough, or singing a clear vowel. (A singer who is

struggling in the head register typically avoids singing a clear [o] or [u], consciously or not.)

- Although the body must gradually increase the efforts of expansion in ascent, the vowel should remain stable at this dynamic level and pitch area. An extra lift of the body at the transition pitch is needed so as not to push through the transition, which would hamper the receptivity to head voice. The extra effort in the body prevents strain in the throat. It helps to maintain a smooth vocal line through the transition.
- The jaw should be loose but not deeply dropped in this pitch range.
- Do not go much beyond the primary transition for now. The upper range is explored in the next chapter.

As addressed in the chapters on resonance and articulation, the [o][e] and [u] [i] are dark/light pairs that possess common resonance properties. Beginning with the [u] in figure 6.11b and the [o] in figure 6.11c should provide rich models for the bright [i] and [e] that follow, vowels that could become tight and thin rather than rich and bright.

- Although the [i] and [e] on the fourth note of the first measure should retain the darkness of the preceding vowels, brightness will almost surely be added if the tongue is in its proper position as forward as possible. A singer does not have to choose between brightness and richness.
- When moving from vowel to vowel, change as little as possible in body and throat. The movements of tongue and lips should be made as loosely as possible and should not hamper consistent resonance. The mouth should be relaxed with no spread of its position. The jaw should be loose but not deeply dropped. Maintain an uninterrupted flow of tone throughout the vocalizations.
- With intentionality, maintain the Open Throat and increase the Open Body while ascending.
- Take the vocalization up by half steps. As it gets higher, the [o] should move toward an [u] formation to encourage more head voice. This must be accompanied by a more energized lift and expansion of the body, or the larynx will rise and the throat will get tight.

An ascending line on a single vowel as in figure 6.11d–e often requires some modification of the vowel to encourage a free entrance into head voice.

- Prepare the singer's body for figure 6.11d–e.
- In figure 6.11d, begin with a rich [o], and ascend the scale while increasing the efforts of body expansion. As you move closer to the primary transition, move toward an [u] formation but not to the point of losing an [o] identity.
- Similarly, in figure 6.11e, the [e] will have to morph slightly toward an [i] as you near the top pitches but without losing the [e] identity and without spread on either vowel. As you begin the vocalization, recall the richness

that the [o] imparted to it in figure 6.11c and begin with that quality. If you need to insert the [o] in front of the [e] to recapture that, do so.

- Move up the scale by half steps in both vocalizations, making the appropriate modifications of vowel and going just past the primary transition but not yet beyond.
- Try this a second time with slightly more volume. This requires even more outward pull of the body and more abdominal participation to fuel the volume. Never let the abdominal participation jeopardize the outward pull of the rib cage. You may need more jaw drop for the louder volumes. Head voice can enter only if the outward pull is maintained. Otherwise, pushing ensues.

EXERCISE

The vocalizations of figure 6.12 continue to encourage head voice access but now with the [ɑ], the least receptive vowel. However, with the Open Body and Open Throat and with the help of slight vowel modification, it too can be coaxed into head voice whenever needed.

Figure 6.12.   Accessing the head voice with [ɑ].

- Choose a comfortable pitch that takes you close to your primary transition at the top of the vocalization but not above it. For all voice types, the top note should be sung fairly softly with a heady quality before trying for more volume.
- The lift in the body assists in making the transition and results in a sensation of lightness in the tone. This is not the same as thinness. The light quality, as opposed to thinness, must include some richness and be free of strain. Richness is an essential element of all vowels in head voice but is allowed only if the larynx is kept low by way of an Open Body and Open Throat.
- For the vocalization of figure 6.12a, encourage more head voice as you ascend the scale by increasing the energized lift of the body and moving the [o] toward a more closed position on top, as suggested in a previous vocalization.
- Do not accent the top note or let it get louder than the lower notes.

- When you move from the [o] to the [ɑ], change the position of the articulators only as much as is needed to create an identifiable [ɑ]. Merely relax the pursed lips and the lift of the tongue. Move the [ɑ] toward a more relaxed vowel, such as [ʌ], as in but, especially as you get higher in the scale and increase the jaw drop.

Trap: The [ʌ] should not become muddy or swallowed sounding, which might be the result of a clutching soft palate. Such extraneous tension hinders free pharyngeal and mouth resonance. Along with the lift of the body, maintain Forward Articulation.

- As you descend on the [ɑ], maintain the heady, mellifluous quality. Maintaining the lift of the body and singing in a smooth unbroken line should prevent it from becoming too heavy or losing its flexibility.
- Now sing the vocalization with an increase in volume. Follow most of the same guidelines as for the softer dynamic, except that both vowels will need more drop of the jaw to accommodate the louder volume especially as the pitch rises. Make sure that the jaw opening is vertical, with no spread of the mouth position.
- Figure 6.12b uses only [ɑ] except for one passing [o]. Approach the top note delicately, with no accent. Allow the jaw to drop more deeply with higher pitches and greater volume.
- Take the vocalization up by half steps until you just pass the primary transition. Experiment with different volume levels, and allow the jaw to drop more deeply at the top. Don't go any higher for now.
- When you have experienced increased headiness on the ascent, omit the [o] from figure 6.12b, and sing the entire vocalization on the [ɑ], recapturing the headiness that had been accessed with the help of the [o].

Strengthening the Head Voice

The rather soft dynamic level of several of these vocalizations has encouraged access to head voice. This is an important step, but head voice may still need strengthening. The following vocalization is designed to encourage more volume in head voice without vocal strain. This work is similar to the work of the female in building the head voice with octave jumps that mirror the strength of the chest voice. However, because it is easier for the male to enter head voice with softer dynamics and darker vowels, it is more effective to add volume *after* head voice has been accessed.

EXERCISE

Figure 6.13.   Adding volume to head voice.

The rhythms of figure 6.13 are designed to encourage a heady approach to the [ɑ], but they are not mandatory. Give yourself time anywhere you like if you need to observe the kinesthetic sensations more closely.

- Prepare for singing with an Open Body and Open Throat, posture erect.
- In figure 6.13, take the rich [o] up, lifting the body as you ascend. Morph into the [ɑ] softly without accenting it and delaying the *crescendo* until after you cross the bar line. Maintain the richness of the [o] as you add the brightness of the [ɑ]. Keep in mind that the higher you go with this, the more important verticality becomes in your vocal framework, the low larynx, dropped jaw, and vertical mouth opening.
- Once you begin the *crescendo*, take it to as much volume as is comfortable. Increasing the volume takes more breath pressure, and this must be monitored with increased efforts of expansion so that push does not ensue. (Recall the muscular antagonism discussed in chapter 4, on resonance.)
- As you increase the volume on [ɑ], increase the body expansion and jaw drop.
- Once you have established a full-bodied [ɑ], slowly take that vowel up two more steps with full volume, substantially increasing the efforts of expansion and jaw drop with each step. When you descend on the last two notes, do so without losing any volume, richness, or expansion. If you are secure with that, you may add the fermata on the highest note in the vocalization.
- Take this vocalization up the scale by half steps until you pass the primary transition by a half step or so but not higher yet.
- Sing this vocalization on other vowels to experience their different behaviors.

Relationships between the Male Chest, Middle, and Head Voice

As with the female voice, once a strong head voice has been achieved, it can be used as a model for pitches in the middle range. The next step, then, is to take that full head voice down the scale into the chest voice territory without completely giving up the strong but heady quality achieved at the top. Maintaining the body expansion is an important factor in that.

EXERCISE

The vocalization in figure 6.14 begins with the challenge of the [ɑ] before allowing the other vowels to enter.

Figure 6.14.   Bringing strength down.

- Choose a starting pitch ensuring that the top pitch is at or just below your transition pitch.
- Encourage as much head voice as possible from the first pitch on, and enter the top note softly on the [ɑ] to preserve the heady quality.
- Once the heady [ɑ] is reached, begin a *crescendo* on it. Without losing the richness or Forward Articulation of that vowel, drop the jaw vertically more and more as you *crescendo*. Increase the efforts of expansion including the depth experienced with the lowered diaphragm and larynx.
- Without losing the fully grounded volume, begin the downward descent. Singing loudly at any pitch level requires more jaw opening and greater efforts of expansion than singing softly. However, as you enter the middle of your range, the jaw drop may not need to be as great as when nearer the primary transition.
- Depending on where you began, you may be moving to or through both the preparatory area and the area just below that. Try to carry the strong but heady sound down all the way, not abandoning the lift of the body as you enter chest voice territory. If you don't maintain the lift, the chest voice is likely to become less mellifluous, and there may be a break of some kind in the tone. Maintaining a smooth line will help, not allowing any interruption of the tonal flow.
- Toward the end of the vocalization, as you add the other vowels, maintain the volume, intensity, and jaw drop according to your volume level.
- If doing this whole vocalization on one breath is problematic for you, you can do one of two things. You can rush through the first chord outline a bit, or you can take an optional breath after the first beat of the third measure as indicated. If you choose to do the latter, make sure that you do not accent the second beat. Whether you take a catch breath or not, make sure that

you maintain the Open Body and Open Throat as it was originally set up throughout the whole vocalization.

- Take this vocalization up and down by half steps, making note of any adjustments that must be made to keep the vocal line smooth and consistent.
- When you have found success with starting on an [o], remove that vowel from the vocalization, but maintain the same preparatory progression to head voice.

EXERCISE

Most of the work so far has focused on developing strength in the head voice and taking that heady strength down into chest voice territory. Maintaining a heady quality in the preparatory area and the pitches below gives warmth and fluidity to the voice even when singing at a loud dynamic.

The following exercise shifts focus from strong and loud singing to a more delicate quality in the chest voice territory. As you might guess by now, it requires a higher proportion of head voice, a lighter mechanism, than a full-voiced chest voice. The three vocalizations are similar and are treated together in the following guidelines.

Figure 6.15. Taming the chest voice (male version).

- Start on a pitch that is just below your primary transition, at the upper end of the preparatory area. Take a slow tempo.
- Begin the [m o] at a moderately soft dynamic level, and morph into the [a], losing no richness. Make sure not to close any pharyngeal space when singing the [m] or the subsequent vowel.
- Take the [a] down the scale, never losing the lift of the body as you move toward the [u] [i] or [e] on the last note of the first full measure. Be sure there is no mouth spread on the [i] or on the [e].
- Morph back into the [a] on the first beat of the last measure and begin the alternations with either the [u] [i] or [e], as indicated in figure 6.15. All vowels must be sung as a single sustained tone rather than as separate tones.
- Maintain the soft heady quality throughout without emphasizing the upper notes in the last measure. (Placing the closed vowels on the upper notes

should help you with that. When you experience a smooth line and consistent resonance on these vowels, you might try putting an [ɑ] on the upper notes. Maintaining their role as connectors without stress might be slightly more difficult with this vowel.)

- Take the vocalization down by half steps, into chest voice territory, while maintaining the soft heady quality. You might want to do a little noodling toward the lower end.
- At this soft volume and in this range, the jaw will not have to be opened more than for speech. Of course, the body and throat must still assume the singer's position! However, as you go down the scale, the degree of effort can lessen somewhat.

THE *MESSA DI VOCE* FOR MALE AND FEMALE VOICES

The vocalizations in figures 6.1–6.15 were designed to encourage the development of the chest voice and head voice by first isolating the registers, particularly those that were the most problematic, and then by blending them. Throughout, flexible adjustments in the body, throat, and vowel have been key ingredients of proper registration.

Developing register blends accomplishes much more than just bridging the "break" that might occur at a transition or matching tones an octave apart. They enable subtle adjustments needed for scales, varying vowels, pitches, and dynamics. A change of volume without any change of pitch or vowel might also require registration adjustments to maintain consistent tonal quality.

Volume-Dictated Adjustments

The following exercises specifically demonstrate the relationship between volume level and registration. They are used to demonstrate how a single vowel on a single pitch can incorporate the full continuum of registration from chest to blend to head, based on volume alone. An increase of volume with a *crescendo* followed by a decrease in volume with a *decrescendo* constitutes a *messa di voce*.

The kinesthetic experience of the following exercises is similar for both males and females. The closer the singer gets to the primary transition, the more difficult it is to maintain a smooth vocal line in a *messa di voce*.

To begin these exercises, choose a pitch comfortably below the primary transition, a pitch on which you can immediately accomplish a smooth line throughout the *crescendo* and *decrescendo*. Only after you find success in that pitch area should you move closer to the transition.

Keep in mind the suggestions previously given about the need for greater efforts of expansion and increased jaw drop at higher volumes, especially in transition areas.

EXERCISE

The vocalization in figure 6.16 begins low, roughly a fourth below the primary transition, and works upwards. It employs the [o] [e] [i] and [u]. The guidelines apply to them as a group while noting differing characteristics.

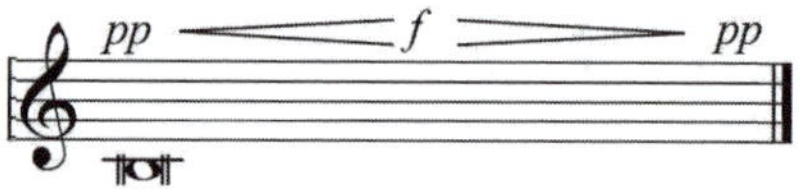

Figure 6.16. *Messa di voce* on four vowels.

a. [o   ]
b. [e   ]
c. [i   ]
d. [u   ]

- Choose a pitch on which it is relatively easy for you to sing both loudly and softly.
- Prepare the Open Body and Open Throat.
- Begin with a soft heady tone on either the [o] [e] [i] or [u] as notated in figure 6.16.
- At softer volumes, the jaw can be relaxed, not opened much, and the lift of the body should be relatively easy until the volume increases to *forte*.
- As you increase the volume, increase the intensity of body expansion even as the abdomen becomes more vigorously involved in providing the air pressure. Maintain the Open Throat for all vowels. As you increase the volume, more chest voice is required than when you are singing softly, but never with push or squeeze in the body.
- Execute the dynamic progression gradually rather than with any abrupt surges. As you get louder, you will need to incorporate more chest voice, and as you get softer, you will need more head voice. A continuum of registration adjustments is needed to facilitate a smooth vocal line not unlike that needed for scales. The jaw opening flexes with the volume: less in soft singing and more in loud singing.
- Move the vocalization up the scale by half steps. Going back and forth between soft and loud singing may become more difficult the closer you get to the primary transition. However, this is easier to do with these vowels than with the [ɑ]. At the primary transition, you need to lighten the register while maintaining richness as you approach head voice territory.

Trap: Do not confuse "lightening" with "thinning." You should experience the richness of your full sized musical instrument throughout the *messa di voce*. The lift of the body helps to keep the throat open and larynx down, requirements for lightening the tone without thinning it.

At this point, if the transition is not as smooth as you would like, don't worry. With time and with better breath management, the muscles will respond to the intention.

EXERCISE

Before we leave the *messa di voce*, the [ɑ] needs to be confronted. It is the vowel that is most likely to lack the qualities that would identify it as a "trained" sound, such as core intensity, clarity, focus, spin, and/or ring. One might conclude that for whatever reason, the [ɑ] is more vulnerable to weaknesses in the system of the Open Body, Open Throat, and Forward Articulation.

In figure 6.16, closed vowels are used to encourage a blend with head when in the softer dynamic and a blend with chest when in the louder dynamic. In the vocalization of figure 6.17, only the [ɑ] is used. It begins softly in a heady quality and makes a *crescendo* through the first measure and over the first bar line as it adds chest voice to the blend. After the [ɑ] reaches full volume, it "noodles" around the central pitch at that volume before it begins the final *decrescendo*.

Figure 6.17. The strong mellifluous [ɑ].

- Prepare the singer's body.
- Choose a pitch that is comfortably below the primary transition.
- Begin the [ɑ] softly in a head voice mode, *crescendo* to *forte*, while maintaining a warm quality at the peak of volume. Forming it in a vertical framework prevents it from spreading. Maintaining the lift of the body keeps some head quality in the chest–head mix, even as the percentage of chest voice increases. Do not push!
- As the volume increases, open the jaw more and more deeply.

- As you do the noodling as indicated, be sure to maintain volume for the entire second measure but without emphasizing the upper notes. Maintain a strong, smooth, unbroken line.
- As you make the *decrescendo*, the body and jaw can relax somewhat but without losing the active lift of the body.
- Move up the scale by half steps. Going back and forth between soft and loud singing becomes more difficult the closer you get to the primary transition. Meeting this challenge requires still more lift of the body and more jaw drop at the more voluminous part of the *crescendo*.

SUMMARY

The exercises presented here are in no way comprehensive, nor are they the only path to mastering the principles of registration. However, they should clarify the function of registers and the means of enabling registration shifts with adjustments of the body, throat, volume, and vowel. The ideal voice is fully grounded in an Open Body and Open Throat and utilizes the full spectrum of chest, middle, and head voice in varying proportions. Fluid registration shifts allow an even vocal line from the bottom to the top of the range with varying vowels and dynamic levels.

The chest voice can strengthen and beautify the head register, and the head register can add flexibility and warmth to the chest voice. This synergy contributes to a substantial middle voice. All three working together in a delicate and flexible balance allow the voice to function as one instrument with a broad tonal palette.

The simplest possible exercises were chosen to demonstrate the principles of registration most clearly as they are experienced by the singer. The skills learned by doing them mindfully are foundational and can facilitate more complicated vocalises and musical challenges. The guidelines for the exercises were customized for each vocalization and are detailed, but they are all grounded in the Three Steps. With additional discernment, they can be counted on to refine the voice as much as to build it. The OOFing mantra is one way of maintaining focus on the Three Steps, all of which are integral to developing refined skills.

If you haven't yet achieved mastery at gracefully negotiating the primary transition, be assured that it takes some time to integrate the Open Throat and Open Body with the flexibility needed. However, every day of practice should make some tangible headway in the process. Applying the principles of registration in these exercises should help your muscles become more responsive to your intentions.

Gaining skills with the Three Steps has been well served by staying in the middle range up to this point, and it has prepared the way to developing the upper range, the subject of the next chapter. The principles of registration play an important role in that development.

The continuing discussion and layering expand in direct proportion to the expansion of the vocal range. The Three Steps will be at the core as always. Ever onward.

· 7 ·

Developing the Upper Range

$\mathcal{F}$or singers to take their skills to higher levels and be able to sing demanding repertoire, they must increase their vocal range to at least a two-octave range. The upper range might be the most demanding area of the voice, but it must be sung with seeming ease. This requires the integration of the Three Steps as detailed in part II, along with registration facility as detailed in the previous chapter. Taking skills to greater refinement—the purpose of part III—requires fine tuning.

As with developing registration facility, developing the upper range does not require new skills but, rather, refined tools of discernment in the use of the basic Three Steps. The OOFing mantra, and all that it implies, continues to be foundational and will continue to appear both in the contextual explanations and in the guidelines for the vocalizations.

The discussion of registration in the last chapter included work in chest, middle, and head voice. The focus for men was on accessing the head voice through the preparatory area leading up to the primary transition. The focus for women was on developing the chest voice and relating it to middle and head. Exercises took the singer only a step or so into the upper range. While that was a limited foray into the upper range, it was crucial preparation for further development in range extension. In fact, if you have assimilated the principles of registration built on the Three Steps, you have come most of the way toward developing your upper range with strength and freedom. This chapter now expands on that.

The underlying principles for developing the upper range for men and women are basically the same, but there are enough differences to warrant separate treatments in this chapter. Male and female singers alike must take into consideration matters of breath, jaw, and vowel when approaching the upper range, but exactly how they use the breath, jaw, and vowel may differ depending on any number of things, especially pitch. This is explained further in the context section. Many of the exercises offered are similar for both genders, but the order of presenting them and the guidelines suggested for their execution vary somewhat.

The male's upper range, primarily in head voice territory, is probably the least developed area of his voice since most of his vocal range falls in chest voice territory. Although the female's upper range falls primarily in head voice territory, as does most of her singing, the upper range is nonetheless particularly demanding. For both male and female, the upper range is often the most challenging, more so than it needs to be.

THE CONTEXT

This section is meant to provide a brief explanation of the premises upon which the exercises for developing the upper range are built. Their clarification should enhance the singer's experience with them.

As demonstrated in the last chapter, the chest, middle, and head voice mutually benefit one another in both male and female voices when they are properly developed. The upper range in all voices is primarily dependent on the head register but in varying relationships to the total vocal range. The evenness of the vocal line throughout the range is a composite of all possible registration adjustments available to the singer. Such adjustments don't stop at the entrance to the upper range but continue to the uppermost reaches of your vocal range with ever-increasing energy from the Open Body and Open Throat. Forward Articulation remains important in the upper range, but varying degrees of vowel modification are needed to maintain ease in that pitch area.

I have spoken of "verticality" in earlier chapters and with increasing frequency. It becomes still more important when moving into the upper range. Verticality is both a sensation and a description that comes from the physical reality of an open vocal tract, a vertical one initiated with the lowered diaphragm, enhanced with the lowered larynx, and extending up through the pharynx, mouth, and sometimes nose. It is manifested by the vertical movements and formations of jaw drop, mouth, and vowel. It counteracts a horizontal framework reflective of a high larynx, tight jaw, and spread mouth. In this mode, rather than fostering a free vocal tract and the flow of free tone, tone is inappropriately entwined with the throat. Fortunately, the physical movements and formations needed to create a vertical framework can be directly controlled.

Skills with negotiating registers and managing the breath are crucial factors in the ability to sing high with ease and full resonance. Specifically, singing in the upper range requires greatly increased efforts of expansion to allow the vocal folds to assume and keep the increasingly long and thin shape required of the highest pitches. Without proper breath management, the natural tendency is to push with the in-and-down muscles, causing the vocal folds to resist and the larynx to rise. Because of the crucial relationship between breath and the upper range, exercises in this chapter are built on a secure kinesthetic experience of the Open Body.

I am reminded here of a woman I agreed to teach as a favor to a friend. The woman sang in a church choir and had recognized that certain anthems posed obstacles for her, especially those that required pitches above her comfort zone. What she wanted to get from her lessons with me was the skill of singing those higher pitches. So as usual, in the first two lessons, I gave her the real deal by going through the issues of posture and then the Three Steps. Although all singers need these basics, she desperately needed them, as her posture was poor, her breath system in a grunt mode, and her tone strident. By the third lesson, just as I was wondering if I had taken on more than I had bargained for, I could tell that she too was frustrated. She exclaimed, "But I wanted you to teach me how to sing high!" I responded as sympathetically as I could, "That's exactly what I'm doing—by working with your body, breath, and tone." It was more than she had bargained for, and we decided to cease the lessons—all in good spirit, thank goodness. I had no magic bullet for singing high, only a process.

The ease with which tone can be produced improves the quality of tone anywhere in the vocal range. By making the breathing muscles carry the workload of the upper range, the throat is saved from having to compensate with extraneous tensions. Without proper breath management, the Open Throat cannot be achieved, and the vocal mechanism is forced to work hard with poor results. To say the least, this limits the upper range. Proper breath management for the upper range simply means increasing the efforts of expansion as you go up the scale. It's that simple. It's foundational. The importance of this was highlighted in the last chapter when greater efforts of expansion sometimes called a "lift" accommodated the primary transition and preparatory area. It becomes even more important as the singer goes further into the upper range.

The opening of the jaw is also crucial in the upper range more so than in lower pitch areas. Singers must deeply drop their jaws as they ascend the scale or increase the volume. How and when this is done varies from male to female, so this is addressed more specifically in the individual exercises to follow. Discernment of the amount of jaw drop needed is based on the particular musical context, but as a rule, all voices need a deeply dropped jaw when singing voluminously in the upper range.

The role of vowels in accessing head voice played an important role in the last chapter. For instance, [o] and [u] were particularly helpful in this regard because of their natural propensity to incorporate head register earlier than [ɑ]. Of course, an arbitrary choice of vowels is not always possible when text specifies the words that must be articulated. However, judicious modifications of vowels that borrow the natural properties of other vowels can lend ease and freedom to otherwise difficult pitches in the upper range. This can often be done without losing the identity of the given vowel. Modification is required at different pitches on different vowels for male and female voices. How it will synch with the opening of the jaw also differs between male and female voices. While these elements of vocal technique are not new—they are explored in parts I and II—they now require greater discernment as to how/when they are used.

Considering the importance of finessed breath management, it might be helpful to clear up two terms often associated with the breath: "energy" and "pushing." These terms are commonly heard in and out of the voice studio and are mentioned in this book. They are commonly subject to misconceptions and misapplications.

Singers often mention energy when I ask them how they breathe for singing. Of course, I then ask what they mean by energy, and it's clear that more times than not, they have no idea what energy is, where it is located, or how it is used. This is true for advanced singers as well as less developed singers. While more energy in the system of breath management is needed for singing in the upper range, I think one has to be careful with throwing that word around loosely. Not all energy is equal. It takes a lot of energy, for instance, to push a voice, but this is not the kind of energy needed for good singing. Terms need to be defined.

Maintaining cultivated simplicity of terminology for the sake of clarity, allow me to offer my working version of the term "energy." Whenever it is used with the following exercises, it refers to the efforts of the out-and-up lift of the body in preparation to sing and the continuing efforts while singing. Sometimes these efforts are referred to as "engaging the body" or "keeping the body engaged," but there is much

Trap: As before, the "out-and-up" pull is somewhat abbreviated, lacking reference to the downward sensation of the lowering diaphragm. I use this shortened form for the sake of brevity even though I think the "down" part is often exaggerated and not really related to filling the lungs with air. The kinesthetic experience of inhalation, the Open Body, is initiated by the lowering of the diaphragm, completed by the expansion of the thorax, and instrumental in creating the Open Throat.

misunderstanding about those terms, too. The energy or engagement that keeps the out-and-up muscles active is quite different from the efforts that squeeze the body with in-and-down muscles, indicative of pushing.

Curiously, when singers refer to pushing, they often gesture to their throat and say something like "I know I'm pushing in my throat." I find this interesting because there are no mechanisms in the throat to push. What the singers are actually experiencing in the throat is constriction, most likely caused by the swallowing muscles as a reaction to the body squeezing. It is all too similar to grunting, not amenable to singing free tones.

Having laid out the premises of developing the upper range and clearing up some terminology, this discussion begins with the male voice. Nowhere else is the strain of singing up the scale quite as glaring as in a male who is not adept at using the head voice register. This is most common in high school and young college-age singers, of course, but in advanced singers, it is often manifested as tensions, strain, and limitations in the upper range. While part II limits all exercises to the middle range and the exercises in the registration chapter only venture nominally into the upper range, exercises in this chapter take the singer up to and well into the upper range.

As before, only a handful of vocalizations are presented here, not much more elaborate than exercises in previous chapters. They were chosen for the directness with which they highlight a particular element of technique needed to sing in the upper range. They are presented in a methodical, step-by-step manner that details a kinesthetic process for using the body to serve freedom and full resonance in the upper range. The suggested starting pitches are mere suggestions but should serve most voice types. If you are able to find more success with a slightly different starting pitch, do so. Guidelines are offered to help you choose the best pitch.

As always, the guidelines are customized for each exercise so that the particular challenges and goals of each one are addressed directly. Lest you feel burdened with the detail of the guidelines, keep in mind that they all fall under the umbrella of the Three Steps. The OOFing mantra should keep that clear.

THE MALE UPPER RANGE

As in previous chapters, developing a specific skill is best served by deconstructing the process, slowing it down, and building it from the ground floor up. I cannot stress enough the importance of a mindful approach to these exercises. They are kinesthetic experiences that can enable successful vocalizations rather quickly. However, consistency of application takes time. This involves training muscles, and muscle memory has its own time table. In the meantime, your success depends on mind over matter.

Being that quality is more productive than quantity for skill refinement, you might want to do only one or two exercises at a single practice session. The intention in your practice should be to integrate each exercise with the Three Steps. The guidelines should be helpful for this. They focus on the Open Body, Open Throat, and Forward Articulation rather than on the tone. If the physical foundation is good, the tone will be good.

EXERCISE

The upper range demands a strong and secure head register. The simple scales in figure 7.1 incorporate the [o] and [e] because of their receptivity to the head register. The more closed nature [u] and [i] have similar receptivity, but at this point, they are likely to inhibit the deeply dropped jaw that must be encouraged for the upper range.

The nasal semivowel [m] precedes the [o] as a means of encouraging verticality with tone that is directed up the nasopharynx, the highest section of the pharynx. Furthermore, because the tone exits through the nose, it causes a buzz there, as well as in the gently closed lips. This encourages the Forward Articulation of both the [o] and [e] but only if the expanded body is prepared well and maintained during singing.

Figure 7.1.   Scales on [o] and [e].

The suggested starting pitch in this exercise is probably more suited to lower voices, but some tenors may find it useful in that the upper notes might be the beginning of the preparatory area. These vowels are particularly receptive to head voice, especially at a moderately soft volume, so the preparatory area is likely to be lower than expected.

- With a singer's posture, prepare the Open Throat and Open Body with a yawning breath.
- Be sure that the [m] is formed with a loose closure of the lips with no impingement on the mouth or pharyngeal space.
- As you begin the vocalization, do not allow any loss of lift or expansion of the body.
- As you ascend the first five pitches with the vowels indicated, increasing the lift of the body with each step becomes important early but particularly

toward the top. Remember that to some degree, each pitch in the scale requires its own register adjustment. This is enabled by increased energy of expansion efforts, as this prevents excessive force on the vocal folds.

- Low voices may need to close the vowel slightly toward [u] on the upper pitch to encourage head voice. Doing so should create a darker color at the top (sometimes called "cover") as opposed to a thin, spread, or pushed tone.
- The [e] should be treated similarly as it nears the top, closing slightly toward the [i]. In either case, the slight modification should be synchronous with the extra lift of the body.
- Make sure that the [e] is formed in a vertical framework, a dropped jaw, with no spread of the mouth. The vowel template is managed solely by a loose tongue moving into the appropriate positions.
- Take this vocalization up by half steps, increasing the body lift at the transition.
- Go well beyond the primary transition as long as you can do so without strain in the throat. However, it is quite alright to feel the extra workload in the body. Increased outward directed energy is required of an ascending scale.
- As you go higher in your upper range and if you are increasing volume, gradually drop the jaw incrementally farther, even if you are choosing a slightly more closed vowel toward the top of the range. Use the amount of jaw opening that allows freedom in the vocal tract, more for louder singing, less for softer singing.
- Sing the vocalization at different volume levels. The more voluminous, the greater the jaw drop, abdominal involvement, and energy of expansion.
- Continue to the top of your upper range or until you become aware of strain in the throat. The Open Body is the working servant of a free Open Throat.

EXERCISE

The vocalizations of figure 7.2 are modifications of the one in figure 7.1. It incorporates the [ɑ], which is slightly less receptive to the head register than the other vowels. To ameliorate this, the [o] and [e] are placed in front of the [ɑ] as a model for the headier, richer quality.

- For figure 7.2, prepare the Open Throat and Open Body with a yawning breath.

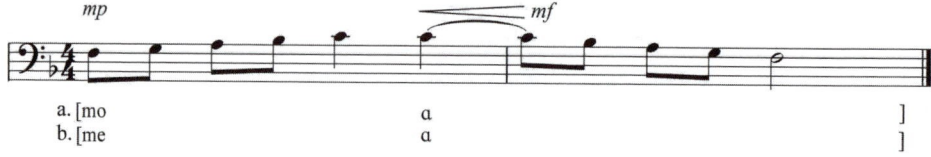

Figure 7.2. Scales including [ɑ].

- For figure 7.2a, follow the guidelines for figure 7.1 with regard to beginning on [mo].
- Follow the guidelines for figure 7.1 relative to approaching the ascending stepwise scale.
- On the fourth beat of figure 7.2, morph into the [ɑ] with no accent, releasing the pursing of the lips and avoiding any spread of the mouth. The [ɑ] should reflect the richness of the [o] without losing the [ɑ] identity. Both vowels should be formed in a vertical framework.
- All notes should be sung as a single continuous tone rather than as separate tones.
- The upward scale should not increase in volume. Maintain the *mp* until the *crescendo* begins on the fourth beat of the first measure, continuing across the bar line.
- Assuming that the [ɑ] has incorporated some of the heady richness of the [o], take care not to lose this mellifluous quality as you descend the scale, even while maintaining the increased volume level.
- Beginning with [m e] in figure 7.2b, avoid any mouth spread. The [e] and [o] possess similar properties of richness even though the [e] adds brightness to the tonal color.
- Morph from the [e] to the [ɑ], maintaining the verticality in both vowels and thinking of them as one continuous tone with two colors.
- Continue to follow all the guidelines for figure 7.2a.
- Take the vocalization up by half steps and explore the topmost reaches of your upper range, increasing the energy of expansion and jaw drop with each note up. Do not go further if you feel strain in the throat.

EXERCISE

A broken chord outline, the *arpeggio,* is a familiar vocalise to singers. It can cover the span of an octave or more and can assume many different forms. The vocalizations in figure 7.3 cover the span of an octave and once again make use of the [o] and [e] as a model for the [ɑ]. The semivowel [n] is used with much the same goals of the [m] in previous vocalizations with its high and forward breath flow and its capability to sustain pitch. However, instead of closed lips directing the breath in that direction, it is the contact between the lifted tongue and the upper roof of the mouth behind the

Figure 7.3.   *Arpeggio* (male version).

upper front teeth that prevents the tone from exiting the mouth. Therefore, there is not as much open space in the mouth as there is behind the [m]. Be aware of this and make sure it does not constrict the pharyngeal space. If you experience constriction, feel free to substitute an [m] for the [n].

The three vocalizations in this group have some common goals. The [n o] and [n e] are used for their natural richness and receptivity to head voice at the beginning of the exercises, on the top pitches, and at the end. The [n a] is surrounded by these sounds in the hopes that it will not spread or lose focus. Once the heady [n o] and [n e] are experienced on the top pitch without emphasis, the [a] is left to its own devices in figure 7.3c.

- With a singer's posture, prepare the Open Throat and Open Body with a yawning breath for figure 7.3.
- Be sure that the [n] is formed with a loose lift of the tongue and that the closure does not negatively affect the mouth space behind the lift or the pharyngeal space behind the mouth.
- As you begin the vocalization on either the [n o] or [n e] and throughout the entire vocalization, maintain the lift and expansion of the body, increasing it as you move upward.
- Morph from the [n o] or [n e] to the [a] with as little movement as possible, limited only to the release of lip pursing and tongue lift. Be sure the [a] is formed in a vertical framework and that it does not have a thinner or less vibrant sound than the [o]. If it loses vibrancy, it very well could be due to a body that is not putting enough energy into the body expansion. Avoid any spread of the mouth, especially on the [n e].

Trap: Often the body expansion tends to weaken when passing through the [a], causing that vowel to lose its verticality and clarity. Although the [a] is passed through quickly, it should be every bit as important as the other vowels and should not spread. This can be maintained by the stable expansion efforts of the body.

- In figure 7.3c, as you take the [a] to the top pitch, you must give an extra lift to your body and drop the jaw a bit farther, especially as you move toward the top of your range. Moving by skips requires incrementally more lift of the body than moving by step. Make sure the skip is smooth with no hint of an [h] in it. Thinking of "drinking in the air" might help you maintain the body's expansion as you ascend, encouraging increased muscular efforts of inhalation (expansion). You should enter the top note with ample volume but without emphasis or accent, and in so doing, you should experience a freer and richer production.

Trap: Many singers tend to stress high notes whether or not that is suggested by the musical context. This reflects pushing up a lower registration rather than gradually incorporating more head voice. The highest pitch can be sung at the same volume as the others but without stress or accent.

- The jaw can relax on the way down, but maintain the lift of the body and the verticality of the [ɑ].
- Take the vocalization up by half steps well through the primary transition, paying special attention to increased body lift at the transition. Proceed as high as you can without strain. This takes much energy in the body to maintain the expansion, but this is distinctly different from vocal strain. The jaw drops more deeply with each step up, especially near the top of the vocal range.
- Sing the vocalization with increased volume.
- At the top of your range, you may find that moving to the vowel [ʌ], as in *but*, might help, but do not allow any clutching in the soft palate. Maintain the deeply dropped jaw.
- At the highest part of your range, there should be ample head register blended into the tone. Take this quality down as you finish the vocalization, brightening the vowel again as you descend.

EXERCISE

The following vocalization is designed to build volume and stamina in the upper range. It first encourages access to the head register before morphing into the [ɑ]. Then a *crescendo* on it goes to full volume in ascent before taking the same volume down two steps. There should be no pushing in your attempt for volume on high pitches, but the abdominals will be more active as the diaphragm and rib muscles cooperate in monitoring the energetic air pressure. As you increase the volume in this area of the voice, chest voice will be incorporated into a chest–head blend, much like what female singers experience in this pitch area when they are using more volume. However, since you are in your upper range, as opposed to the female's middle range, it will require much more outward directed energy in your body as well as jaw drop.

Figure 7.4.   Volume and stamina (male version).

- Prepare as you have for the previous exercises. Begin the vocalization softly.
- Similar to the vocalization in figure 7.3c, when you morph into the first [ɑ], maintain the richness of the [o] with added brightness and in a vertical framework with no accent.
- The entire line should form one continuous, uninterrupted tone.
- Make sure that the second and third notes of the first measure have no hint of an [h] before them. If the Open Body holds, you should be able to sing them in a *legato* manner with a continuous tone with no undue pulses.

- Enter the [ɑ] softly, incorporating a good deal of head register in it. Make sure that the flow of tone is not hampered and that it is just as resonant as the [o]. Until you get higher, you will not need significant jaw drop.
- Take the *crescendo* to the highest level possible without compromising the quality or resorting to push. Your body will have to work harder to feed the tone for more volume and maintain the efforts of expansion. (Recall the muscular antagonism of breath management discussed in chapter 3, on the Open Body.)
- As you move up two more pitches, toward the top of your upper range, you will need to incrementally drop your jaw more deeply with a vertical mouth position. You may find that moving to the vowel [ʌ], as in *but*, might help, but do not allow a muddy vowel with any clutching in the soft palate.
- The head register that you began the vocalization with should not be abandoned as more volume is added. While head register benefits most pitches, it is absolutely necessary for these strong pitches that may now be in head voice territory. However, strength in this area requires the fortification of a chest–head blend. It takes incredible expansion efforts in the body.
- You may hold the top note for a while, or you may choose to "noodle" around it. Do this only if you are maintaining your expansion well and the tone is not strained.
- Take this quality down the last two steps with full volume as you finish the vocalization, never losing the lift of the body.
- Take this vocalization as high as you can do so without strain in the throat.

EXERCISE

The aforementioned vocalizations are all based on a *legato* execution. The next chapter explores *legato* singing in greater depth, but before leaving this section, we must address the techniques of *staccato*. Singing in a *staccato* style requires short accented notes, the opposite of *legato*. Very often when singers sing *staccato*, rather than singing short, fully resonant tones, they sing short, cramped tones. The reason is that the Open Body loses its stable expansion. Instead of relying on abdominal pulses to make the stops and starts required of *staccato*, the ribs and chest take on that role, pulsing for every note. Obviously, the expansion of the body has been compromised, and it cannot serve the Open Throat that way. Resonance suffers.

In the following vocalization, so that the Open Body is not compromised, the stable rib muscles must be isolated from the active abdominal/diaphragmatic muscles.

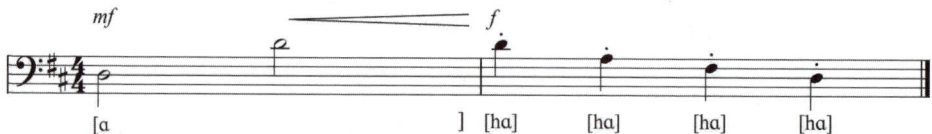

Figure 7.5. Prepared *staccato* (male version).

- Prepare the singer's body.
- Begin with a moderately dropped jaw and volume on [ɑ]. Do not lose any lift of the body no matter how assertively you begin.
- Take the pitch up the octave in a *legato* manner with a volume equal to the first note but without adding volume, stressing, or accenting the upper pitch. This can be accomplished only if the Open Body increases the efforts of expansion as you ascend.
- Make a *crescendo* on the upper pitch, dropping your jaw as the volume increases.
- As you move to the first *staccato* note, anchor the lift of your body so that you do not blow that note through collapse or push. Minimize the aspirate quality of the [h]. As you begin the *staccato* notes, maintain the same jaw drop and body expanse as the last note of the first measure. The abdominal area will pulse but only as much as needed and without involving the chest or ribs. Continue with this physical positioning through all four *staccato* notes. The *staccato* notes should be just as resonant as your most beautiful legato notes. If you would like to check this, sing one of the *staccato* notes, stop, and start again on the same pitch with a sustained tone. The two should be equal in sonority.
- Take the vocalization up the scale by half steps until you have reached the top of your usable vocal range or just beyond, dropping the jaw more and more deeply as you ascend, working the muscles of inhalation with more energy, and modifying the vowel slightly toward [ʌ].

THE FEMALE UPPER RANGE

Since the head voice covers the majority of the female vocal range, accessing it is not so much the issue as finding strength and freedom there. Very often, even if a soprano's upper range is sung with ease, it might lack core, strength, volume, or warmth there. Integrating the Three Steps with registration skills provides balance for the whole voice. It enables consistent tone quality from the lower range through the upper range.

EXERCISE

The following vocalization is a simple *arpeggio*. Similar to exercises for the male voice, it employs [mo] to give a rich heady quality to the lower notes with a forward flow of the breath through the initial nasal consonant. However, unlike the male, the female needs to open her vowels as she ascends the scale.

[mo   ɑ   o   ]

Figure 7.6. *Arpeggio* **(female version).**

- With a singer's posture, prepare the Open Throat and Open Body with a yawning breath.
- Loosely close the lips, but make sure that the mouth and pharynx are opened and air filled.
- As you begin the vocalization, do not allow any loss of lift or expansion of the body. Think of the entire vocalization as a single continuous flow of tone. Give special attention to the lift of the body with every skip upward, or you may be hampering a lighter mechanism (head voice) needed for ascending pitches.
- Morph into the [ɑ] with a lift of the body, without any accent or stress on it. It's important, but you are just passing through it at this point.
- Make sure that an [h] does not creep in before any of the notes. Singers often exaggerate that aspirate consonant, consciously or not, to help them "hit" the next pitch. This is indicative of the pulsing that compromises the Open Body, a version of the squeeze/push mode. It would cause an interruption of the *legato* line and hamper access into a lighter mechanism. Giving the body a continuing "lift" as you ascend should prevent this.
- When you morph to the [ɑ], do so in a vertical framework so that the vowel does not spread. The [ɑ] should not have a thinner or less vibrant sound than the [o].
- At lower pitch levels, the jaw does not need to drop beyond the position used in speech. At the starting pitch level, even the more "open" [ɑ] should not need much jaw drop.
- Increase the Open Body and Open Throat for every pitch up, even though the energy level needed at first will not be high. Do not accent or stress the highest pitch. Rather than singing to the pitch, sing through it. (Refer to the "trap" that details this tendency to stress upper pitches in the guidelines for figure 7.3.) Thinking of "drinking in the air" should help the efforts of inhalation (expansion) to remain active.
- On the way down, morph back into the [o] seamlessly, with the body remaining stable.
- Take the vocalization up by half steps. As you near and cross the secondary transition, the jaw will need to increase the drop and continue to do so in increments as you ascend.
- It is important to form your vowel in a vertical framework the higher you go. This will be aided with a lowered diaphragm and larynx, vertically dropped jaw, and no spread of the mouth. The upper lip should not cover any of the upper teeth, but neither should the lips spread in a smile. Any kind of horizontal formation will limit the top of the range, especially if you go into the

extension above high C. At that point, verticality of the vocal tract becomes most critical, and I sometimes suggest here that the tone must be tall and narrow, enough so that it could thread a needle! (I am confessing to another use of imagery here, I know.) Verticality coupled with an energetic Open Body frees the throat to access these high pitches with ease. The body is working very hard so that the throat is unencumbered.

- When you have gone as high as you can go without strain in the throat, take the vocalization down by half steps without losing the lift of the body. Maintain the *legato* line with consistent volume.
- If you have been singing with moderate volume up to now, sing the vocalization again with increased volume. Note the increase of energy that is required in the abdominals that provide air pressure for loud tones against the gently resisting lowered diaphragm as well as the continuing lift of the rib muscles. Make sure this muscular antagonism does not become static. It must remain flexible while monitoring adequate breath flow.

EXERCISE

Doing quick scales in the upper range allows the voice to be exercised there without taxing it too much. The vowel that is most conducive to the upper range is the [ɑ] as long as the Open Body is maintained with a dropped jaw and sung in a vertical framework. Other vowels will need to modify, more so as the pitch ascends. The [e] will have to modify toward an [ɛ], as in *bet*, the [o] toward an [ɔ], as in *saw*. The [i] is avoided in this vocalization because its resonance properties do not mesh with those of the upper range unless it is modified considerably toward an [ɪ]. Most composers are sensitive to this and don't place the [i] on pitches above the secondary transition. The [u] creates similar challenges and needs to modify toward an [ʊ], as in *foot*. In the upper range, the priority must be a tension-free throat more than a vowel that cannot be sung on those pitches without strain. The pitch, volume, and amount of jaw opening dictate the amount of modification needed.

a.[ɑ   ]
b.[e   ]
c.[o   ]

Figure 7.7.   Scales.

- Prepare the singer's Open Body and Open Throat for the vocalizations of figure 7.7.
- At the suggested starting pitch, the jaw drop need only be loosely and comfortably dropped, not deeply dropped. What is more important is that the

Open Body and Open Throat are poised to resonate any of the three vowels in a vertical framework.

- As you ascend the first five pitches, slightly increase the expansion and take care not to stress the upper pitch. The natural tendency is to push up the scale. This would cause two things: resistance to a lighter registration adjustment and emphasis of a note that should not receive it.
- The [e] and [o] need to incorporate head voice earlier than the [ɑ]. Such adjustment might begin as early as the third or fourth note up the scale. Add some lift to the body, and be sure that the vowels maintain a vertical framework.
- Remember that all vowels are shaped by the tongue and that *none* require a spread mouth position.
- By not emphasizing the upper pitch, you are poised for continuing up the scale because the body expansion has not loosened or resorted to squeezing. This expansion must continue to increase with each step up, requiring much energy in the upper range.
- Take the vocalization up as high as you can energetically sustain at moderate volume, always dropping the jaw farther and being sure the jaw and mouth provide a vertical framework.
- As you ascend, concentrate on the freedom in the throat more than a rigid concept of the vowel. Remember that the least bit of tension is a clue that you should be incorporating more head voice, a lighter register. Vocal strain or diminishment of tone quality, even if slight, are typical indications that either the body is not maintaining its expansion or the vowel template is too rigidly fixed. An increasingly deeper jaw drop should accompany the ascending pitch and contribute to modification.
- Take the vocalization up by half steps until you are well into your upper range. Go as high as you can without vocal strain.
- Finally, sing through all three vowels of figure 7.7 with increased volume, and note the increased energy needed in the body as well as the greater jaw drop.

EXERCISE

Vocalises employing *staccato*, notes that are considerably shortened compared to the same note values in *legato* singing, are commonly heard in voice studios and practice rooms. Even more than scales, they are friendly to the upper range without taxing the voice too much. They encourage flexibility of the abdominal muscles that are largely responsible for the quick starts and stops of tone. However, one should not assume that all *staccato* exercises are aiding a good vocal technique, the following ones included. Just as common as these exercises is the tendency of singers to lose expansion of the body while executing *staccato* notes and to push them out with the in-and-down squeezing muscles. Resonance is impaired, and although this

[mo   a   ]   [hɑ]   [hɑ]   [hɑ]   [hɑ]

Figure 7.8. Prepared *staccato* (female version).

is not as obvious with short notes as long notes, it has deleterious effects on the vocal line. The vocalization in figure 7.8 first prepares a desirable quality of tone on a *legato* ascent before trying for a similar quality on *staccato* notes.

- Prepare the singer's body and throat.
- The first measure is similar to the first measure of figure 7.6. Please use the guidelines for the first four notes of that figure. However, after you arrive at the unstressed upper note, add the *crescendo*.
- As you make the *crescendo*, open the jaw for the added volume, and energize the efforts of expansion.
- At the end of the first measure, as you move into the first *staccato* note, brace the body's expansion in anticipation of the first one. The chest and ribs should remain stable as you sing that note and the others that follow. Those notes should be formed with the same volume, jaw drop, and energy of body expansion as the *legato* tones before it. The abdominals will bounce slightly but only as much as is needed.

Trap: The tendency here is that the first *staccato* is not of the same resonance, space, and volume as the *legato* tones before it. Make sure that the jaw drop that was appropriate for the *legato* tones is maintained in the *staccato* tones and that verticality is consistent. The tendency in *staccato* singing is to lose the down-out-and-up stability of the body and move into an "in-and-down" mode in which the whole upper body is jerkily pulsing out each note. This is often accompanied with upper chest breathing. Exaggerated abdominal pumping is a common trap and one example of unnecessary work being done in the wrong places. You must avoid this and instead allow only your abdomen to do the pulsing, independent of the ever-erect chest and expanded rib cage.

- Although there is an [h] at the start of every note, try to use the aspirated breath sparingly, or you may fall into a blowing mode. You might want to merely *think* of the [h] rather than consciously aspirating it.
- Maintain the volume and the body expansion as you go down the scale on the *staccato* notes, allowing a slight lessening of body energy on the lower pitches but all the while maintaining expansion.
- Take this vocalization up by half steps, going as high as you can go without strain. Remember that at the top of the range, you need to be conscious of verticality with greater jaw drop. Any horizontal formation in the vocal tract limits the range.
- Practice this vocalization until the *staccato* notes can be sung in the same spaces as the *legato* tones, in both body and throat.

EXERCISE

Once you have experienced the cross-pollination of resonant *legato* tones and *staccato* tones, move on to the vocalization of figure 7.9, one without *legato* preparation. This vocalization is familiar to many singers. It covers a wider pitch span and therefore needs continual adjustments of body energy and jaw drop within a single execution of the exercise.

[ha]   [ha]   [ha]   [ha]   [ha]   [ha]   [ha]   [ha]   [ha]   [ha]   [ha]

Figure 7.9. *Staccato* **span.**

- Prepare the singer's body and throat. Be sure there is no body squeeze or collapse on the first note or any subsequent note.
- If done at moderate volume, the first four notes may not need more than a comfortably dropped jaw, but as you move toward the upper note, the jaw needs to incrementally drop farther. On the way down, it should incrementally relax. The Open Body and Open Throat should remain intentionally active throughout.
- As in *legato* exercises, do not stress the upper note any more than the others. Increasing the body's expansion as you move up the scale should help with this.
- Maintain stability in the body. Unlike the notes, the chest and ribs should not be bouncing! Only the abdominal pulsing will reflect the *staccato* nature of the notes.
- Take this to the top of your upper range accommodating those pitches with a deeply dropped jaw.
- You may try this on other vowels, but remember to modify them toward a more open vowel while ascending and to maintain the vertical framework. At the uppermost part of your range, the jaw needs to drop deeply, and all vowels will morph toward [ɑ] or even [ʌ].

EXERCISE

Before leaving this section on exercises for the female upper range, I'd like to return to the octave jumps employed in the last chapter. They encouraged the upper note in head voice to mirror the strength of the lower note in chest voice. After that was established, the upper tone was taken upward but only a step or so beyond the secondary transition. The following vocalization builds on the octave jump but now goes further up the scale well beyond the secondary transition into the upper range. It should be executed with full resonance and strength, all the while maintaining freedom in the vocal tract. Such an exercise builds volume and stamina.

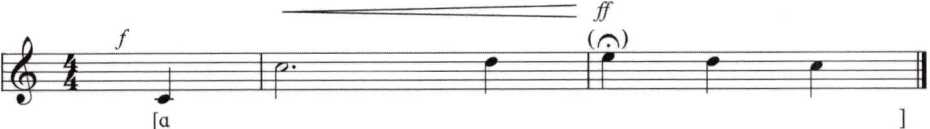

Figure 7.10.   Volume and stamina (female version).

- Prepare the singer's Open Body and Open Throat to sing a voluminous chest tone on the first note. (If you are unable to tap into your chest voice on a C, feel free to start lower.)
- For specific guidelines on executing the octave jump, check back to those offered for figure 6.6 in the last chapter. Suffice it to say here that despite approaching the upper note unabashedly at *forte*, do not let an [h] creep in, as that probably would indicate a push/blow mode in your body rather than an increase of expansion energy. Think of the first and second tones as being one continuous tone on a sustainable vowel. The rest of the vocalization should also be sung in a *legato* manner.
- Make a *crescendo* in the first full measure, gradually increasing the jaw drop and out-and-up efforts.
- Morph into the top note with full volume but with no accent. If you like, you may hold this note for a while, or you could noodle around it as part of stamina development.
- Take this vocalization up by half steps to the top of your upper range as long as it is feeling free in the throat. The body will carry the workload because of the energy needed to sustain *forte* in the upper range. However, the workload does not in any way resemble squeezing or pushing. The energy should be directed outwardly.

SUMMARY

Although men and women function somewhat differently in the upper range, they have more in common than not. Throughout this chapter, I'm sure you have been painstakingly aware of the recurring insistence on correct posture and Three Steps as cornerstones of a good vocal technique. (Anyone who has taught any skill whatsoever understands the need for and value of repetition!) Refined skills with registration and the upper range require new tools of discernment, but they are simply extensions of the fundamental Three Steps. The kinesthetic experience of the unit comprising the Open Body, Open Throat, and Forward Articulation and its extensions is the same for men and women, although the pitch area where they are experienced varies.

There are more commonalities than differences. Allow me to summarize the issues step by step.

Open Body

Both men and women must work in an actively opened body for good breath management. Despite the fact that the upper ranges of men and women are an octave or so apart, they demand the same refinements to enable them to work efficiently. Flexibility is needed in the body so that as the pitch or volume rises, the outward energy in the body increases, and as the pitch or volume decreases, the outward energy lessens somewhat. But never can the efforts of the body relax entirely, or the tone will lose its core. In the upper ranges, the outward energy must increase exponentially to allow the vocal folds to thin and stretch for higher pitches. Never can the efforts of in-and-down muscles take over, or it will result in push, which would create strangling tensions. Refined skills of breath management serve the Open Throat, and this in turn allows free resonance. It also enables registration shifts throughout the vocal range to maintain ease of production and beauty of tone. An even vocal range from chest, through middle, to head voice on, into the upper range is only possible through refined skills of breath management and registration facility.

Open Throat

If the body does its job with breath management and the jaw remains loose, the throat is able to remain flexibly open, free of tensions that would inhibit its resonance potential. Housed within the throat, the vocal folds can function well only as a reaction to the proper conditions provided by proper breath management. With the lowering of the diaphragm and larynx, drop of the jaw, and proper mouth positions, the framework for singing is vertical. Anything short of this detracts from the *chiaroscuro* balance that is possible in the tone. The importance of verticality in the vocal tract is constant.

Forward Articulation

The articulation produced by movements of the tongue, lips, soft palate, and jaw should be as forward as possible. This is important for both males and females in keeping the throat free of unnecessary involvement. However, men and women use vowels differently in different pitch areas. As the male crosses the primary transition, closed vowels help him access head voice, the substance of his upper range. The female enters her upper range an octave above the male's upper range. In that pitch area, she needs to open all vowels, modifying those that do not synch with the high pitches. Both voices need to drop their jaws deeply when singing loudly in the upper range.

The Three Steps remain foundational to all vocal skills, both the basics and the refinements. They continue to hold true for the next chapter, on *legato* singing, which is addressed both as a vocal technique and as an indispensable element of musicality. The two perspectives merge.

· 8 ·

Legato and Musicality

𝓘n part II, the Three Steps—Open Body, Open Throat, and Forward Articulation—were presented step by step as the foundation of a good vocal technique. They focused on the kinesthetic experience of good breath management, resonance, and enunciation with seemingly simple exercises. With added discernment, part III has built on those Three Steps as the means of developing skills with registration and the upper range. This final chapter addresses *legato* singing as a culminating refinement, one that depends on the Three Steps and all refinements enabled by them, not the least of which is finesse with registration.

The word *legato* comes from the Italian word *legare*, which means "to bind or connect." With regard to singing, I'd rather think in terms of connecting the notes rather than binding them. Better yet, the *Harvard Dictionary of Music* (edited by Willi Apel, 1955, 396) offers a definition that includes the following: "to be performed without any perceptible interruption between the notes." This concept has appeared in previous chapters and is at the heart of this chapter.

However, connecting one note to the next smoothly without interruption is not the only requirement of *legato* singing. Singing in a *legato* style requires that all notes in a musical line be sung and connected with the same vocal instrument, a consistent source of resonance. If the singer unduly changes any of the basic elements of vocal production from one note to the next, the instrument changes, and the line is jarred. A lack of consistent resonance detracts from a true *legato*. A vocal instrument that can adjust to pitch, volume, and vowel to enable consistent resonance is the instrument required of *legato* singing. Musicality requires the facility of a well-developed vocal instrument. This is a tall order!

Music theory codifies melody, harmony, and rhythm as the raw materials of musical expression. For the singer, text adds yet another dimension. A vocal line must merge these elements of musical expression in authoritative performance. A major vehicle for that expression is *legato* singing. This chapter addresses the technique of *legato* singing as intrinsically related to musicality. It must serve the music.

Inspiration is a less tangible element of musicality, but high levels of artistry in performance reveal its presence. Inspiration is difficult, if not impossible, to teach, so this chapter does not venture into that territory. However, *legato* singing might well contribute to a singer's inspiration, as it brings the music off the page and into artistry!

The vocalizations in this chapter continue to be rudimentary. They are structured to highlight challenging musical situations as simply as possible. What can be learned through mindful execution of these exercises can be meaningfully applied to more complex music.

THE CONTEXT

It might be beneficial to begin with a review of a few crucial rudiments of music theory but only as relevant to the technique of *legato* singing and its relationship to musicality. I suspect that most readers are familiar with these rudiments, but looking at them through the lens of *legato* singing might lend a new perspective.

Meter

Meter is only one element of rhythm, but it is particularly important for the singer who must express a text. Meter and text often go hand in hand, but it is all too common to hear technically adept singers fail to avail themselves of the suggestions offered by meter. Expressivity suffers because of this. In this sense, what follows is more than an entry-level discussion.

Without musical meter, four spoken expressions of the syllable [l ɑ], all equal in length, would equate to four equal utterances with no indication of weights, direction, or shape. The four spoken syllables in figure 8.1 are unmetered and without specified pitch. Speak it on one continuous tone without emphasizing one note or the other.

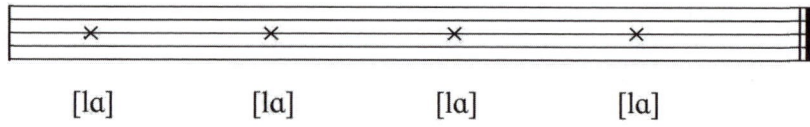

[lɑ]   [lɑ]   [lɑ]   [lɑ]

Figure 8.1.   Spoken syllables without meter.

Speaking in this manner is not only unnatural but quite difficult to do. It is robotic. Life is not robotic and neither is music. Even if the syllables were set to pitched tones, emphasis would not be implicit without meter. Without meter and without text, notes of the same length are equal in all ways. Conversely, in music with meter and words, notes of the same length and the same pitch might look equal, but rarely are they effectively equal.

Meter affects the function and purpose of notes that become expressive largely because of the emphases suggested by meter. For instance, in 4/4 meter, more emphasis is given to the first note, less to the second, slightly more to the third, and still less to the fourth. In figure 8.2, this calibrated weighting is indicated above the staff. The four notes, now in 4/4 meter, are no longer effectively equal.

- Speak the syllables with the weighting accorded to them by the 4/4 meter. Even in speech, you begin to achieve a lilt that involves some subtle changes in

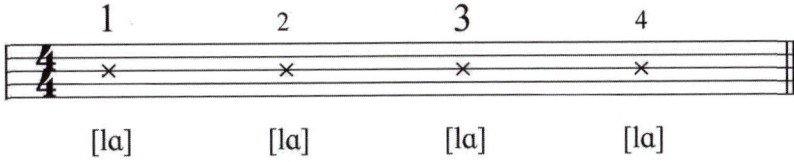

Figure 8.2.   Spoken syllables with meter.

emphasis, volume, and, possibly unwittingly, even pitch. As such, it becomes somewhat musical even without a melody or text.

Words

The specific meaning of words can be expressed through emphasis, even without meter. For instance, a phrase saying "Now I see it" assumes that the dramatic setting gives importance to the words "Now" (as opposed to later) and "see" (as opposed to not seeing). Speaking this line without regard to meter but to only the message would quite naturally reflect the emphases of a metered 4/4 measure as shown in figure 8.3.

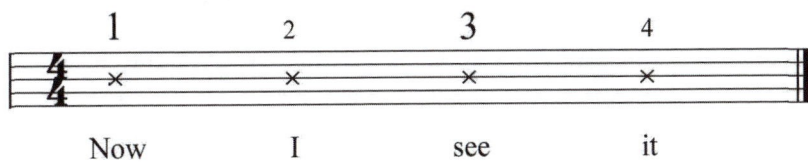

Figure 8.3.   Words and meter.

Most often but not always, text and meter are compatible partners in good music. At other times, in Gregorian chant, for instance, it is the text that provides the points of emphasis, as do subtle pitch changes. In more modern music, when meter is forgone, harmony, rhythm, pitch, and text give indications of emphasis and shape. In French art song, metric weightings are often intentionally blurred, part of a style that reflects the language flow. Singers must utilize any and all musical elements to make relevant decisions about emphases, shape, and direction of musical lines.

This discussion of *legato* is limited to music with a basic compatibility between text and meter, only because in that context it is easier to show the relationship between *legato* and musicality. Text is an important force, even without metric compatibility, and this is transferable to many musical situations.

METER, TEXT, SINGING, AND MUSICALITY

To sing words, not only must the natural stresses of meter and text be carried out, but all skills of vocal technique must be in place. The Open Body, Open Throat, and Forward Articulation must provide a consistently resonant tone on *all* notes, emphasized or not. Notes in a musical line that require less weight or emphasis, such as those that occur on beats two and four in 4/4 meter, must be served with vocal tones that are just as complete and resonant as emphasized notes. "Emphasis," not "volume," is the operative word here. While emphasis may require a momentary increase of volume, notes without emphasis can and often should maintain volume to carry the line forward with strength. They could be included in a *crescendo* and still not be individually emphasized. Notes that don't require individual emphasis should not "come off the voice," nor should they be perceived as "weaker notes." All notes of a phrase should contribute to the *legato* line with consistent tonal core.

Since *legato* singing is the subject of this chapter, the discussion does not focus on accents, of which there are many, including *legato* accents. Although stringing together *legato* and "accent" might seem like an oxymoron, *legato* accents are not percussive accents. For instance, the *tenuto*, indicated with a dash (-) over a note, indicates a weighted emphasis over the whole length of the note, rather than a short, sharp, or percussive accent.

In deconstructing the emphasis of a *tenuto*, a brief and slight *crescendo/decrescendo* (<>) over the note might more nearly assimilate the kind of emphasis that is needed in *legato* singing. Such a subtle *messa di voce* implies a gentle sinking into the center of the note rather than striking it at the start of the note. This delicate emphasis would ensure that the emphasized note could maintain a smooth connection to the notes before and after. *Legato* would not be compromised. More on this later.

In discussing the relationship between text and *legato*, consonants must be addressed as well as vowels. Consonants play a significant role in *legato* singing even with the restrictions they sometimes place on tone. Although some consonants completely stop the tone, such as [k] or [t], others can greatly help *legato* singing. For instance, consonants such as [m] and [n] can carry a sustained tone just as well as vowels. These two can be a great help in connecting one word to another without breaking the line and can bridge the gap of a skip. For instance, in the aria from Handel's *Messiah*, "I know that my Redeemer liveth," achieving *legato* in the skip between the first two notes is considerably helped by giving due resonance to the initial [n] of the second word, "know." While the [n] has the potential of incurring unnecessary tensions in the resonating system, it can be executed freely without impinging on resonance. Done correctly, it is much easier to sing "I know" with a *legato* connection than "I owe," for instance.

As noted in the chapter on articulation, other consonants that can actually enhance *legato* are [l] [v] [w] and [j]. (See the appendix.) Sustainable consonants are your friend! Seize the opportunities they present.

Consonants such as [k] and [t], which offer only noise rather than sustainable sounds, do challenge *legato*, but they possess wonderful expressive potential. Think of what great actors do with consonants! Consonants can spark the drama and provide expressive emphasis. Of course, they must be executed quickly and must be followed with a quick return to unrestricted vowel space.

Notes in a musical line each have a specific function in accordance with text or meter. In my deconstructionist terminology, I have identified them as pick-up notes, framework notes, connectors, or tapered endings. You may not find all of these terms in a music dictionary, but I believe they are helpful in making musical choices that result in beautifully shaped *legato* phrases.

A pick-up is one of the more familiar terms in a musician's vocabulary. The term refers to one or more notes that occur on a weak beat or weak part of a beat and leads to a more emphasized note on a strong beat. Functioning as a gentle introduction to a subsequent note on a strong beat, it can lend elegance and direction to the beginning of phrases. The notes in a phrase that form the bones of the line in terms of melody, harmony, rhythm, and text are the framework notes. They usually occur on strong beats of metered measures and serve as dramatic emphasis in a musical phrase. Although they are the bones of a musical line, singing a phrase with only the bones would result in a sparse, uninteresting, and even awkward musical statement. Other notes are needed to flesh out the musical line as bridges between the framework notes. I refer to these as connectors. They provide *legato* connection and direction that gives momentum to the musical line. Seen in light of this function, they are not "weaker notes" but important ones. They are the unsung—and often neglected—heroes of *legato*! Tapered endings provide the fourth function of notes in *legato* singing. They fall on weak words or syllables, especially at the ends of phrases. The lilt of the text and, usually, the meter are reflected by a mini-*decrescendo*. Tapered endings lend elegance to the endings of phrases, much as pick-ups do at the beginnings of phrases.

Deconstructing a musical line in this way might require some micromanaging in your first attempts at it. Ultimately, the functionally different note types are team players in creating an overarching shape and direction to the musical line. Each note is a unique contributor to that line. As you experiment with identifying the four functions in a musical line, try to progress from a note-to-note mentality toward the overarching shape and flow that they create.

EXERCISE

In the initial discussion about the relationship between text and meter, figure 8.3 shows one way of setting the words "Now I see it" in 4/4 meter. If the meaning of the text were different from that in figure 8.3 and the emphasis needed to be placed on "I" rather than "Now," the metric setting of the words would need to be slightly rearranged. This has been done in figure 8.4, still in 4/4 meter but now with a repeated pitch of choice in your middle range. The example also indicates the four functions of notes as described earlier. Each note is marked with an abbreviated form of a pick-up (*pu*), framework note (*fr*), connector (c), or tapered ending (*te*).

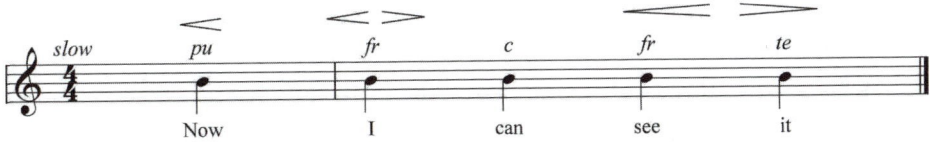

Figure 8.4. Note functions with text and meter.

- Although the framework notes in this vocalization call for emphasis, this need not be exaggerated. The use of dynamics to assist in *legato* emphasis should be subtly executed unless indicated otherwise.
- Prepare the singer's body and throat. Choose a pitch in your middle range. Make sure that the Open Body is maintained through all four note functions.
- Sing the vocalization in a slow tempo.
- Begin the pick-up gently, not attacked with abruptness but glided into. It should make a slight *crescendo* leading toward the downbeat in the next measure.
- Although the word "I" requires a stoppage of tone, called a "glottal attack," make it brief. It automatically lends some emphasis to the tone, but make sure that this emphasis does not include any push from the body. Sink into the tone with a slight mini *messa di voce* for a gentle emphasis rather than a forceful one.
- The next note should continue the strength of the first note but without added emphasis. It should carry the line forward with strength, even with a hint of *crescendo*, primarily through the vowel in the word "can" but also through the final pitched consonant [n].
- The word *see* should take another slight emphasis, and this mini–*messa di voce* merges into the tapered ending (*decrescendo*) entering the word "it."
- Just when you may be thinking that this exercise is much too simplistic, I need to remind you that there are many instances in music where there are repeated notes on the same pitch with the same rhythmic value that are not all equal. When they are sung as equals, it sounds robotic rather than musical. The drama inherent in meter and text must always be reflected in the vocal line.
- Now sing the vocalization as one continuous resonating line. A well-shaped *legato* line can be achieved despite the stoppages that occur with the [k] sound in "can" and the [t] in "it." If your body has remained actively open during their execution, your throat should be able to regain its unrestricted space immediately after these consonants and after the [s] as well.

EXERCISE

In the familiar vocalization of figure 8.5, framework notes alternate with connectors. Because of the skips, issues of registration are involved as well as functionality of the notes. So that the connectors on the upper pitches are not emphasized, a lighter registration needs to be incorporated.

Figure 8.5.   Note functions in a vocalise.

Just as the second and fourth beats should not receive emphasis, the eighth notes within beats in this vocalization should not receive emphasis even though they are the higher ones. However, connectors must maintain consistent resonance. This can happen only if appropriate registration adjustments are enabled with increased efforts of expansion.

Singing units of four eighths rather than units of two will help to maintain movement and direction in the phrase. *Legato* singing is aided by grouping notes together to form larger units. If the notes are sung only as independent entities, momentum will be limited.

- Prepare the singer's body for singing resonant tones with good breath management.
- Beginning on a pitch in your middle range, sing the vocalization in figure 8.5 while paying attention to the function of each note and the phrase shape that emerges. While the focus at this moment in the discussion is on the function of notes within a phrase, the goal is to string them together to create a sweep of the entire line.

Trap: The tendency is to emphasize higher pitches, but in this example, they are all connectors that must maintain consistent resonance without individual emphasis. This requires the lift of the body with each skip up to enable a lighter registration. It does not imply a softer volume. The lift of the body will need to be increased as you ascend, especially if you are near the primary or secondary transition.

- Move the vocalization up by half steps, well into your upper range. Keep in mind the guidelines suggested in the last chapter on the upper range with regard to increasing the energy of expansion and drop of the jaw as well as loosening (modifying) the vowel formations as needed. The female voice has to open the three middle syllables, especially in the upper range. Early modification is not needed as by the male voice until well into the upper range or when volume is substantially increased.
- Sing the vocalization at various volume levels with the OOFing mantra in mind. Maintain *legato* through unstressed but strong connectors that carry the line forward.

MUSIC EXCERPTS

Now that the functions of notes and words in metered phrases have been deconstructed in simple vocalizations, examples from pieces of music should further demonstrate their relevance. The following musical examples are arias from Handel's *Messiah*. The one shown in figure 8.6 is "I know that my Redeemer liveth" for soprano, and the one in figure 8.7 is "The people that walked in darkness" for bass. They were chosen because they are well known, in English, and can serve to demonstrate the role of pick-ups, framework notes, connectors, and tapered endings in a musical context. It is not necessary for the reader to be a soprano or bass to benefit from the exercises, as the functions discussed are applicable to any music in a *legato* style.

If you are a mezzo-soprano, the key given for the soprano aria will most likely work well for you. Singing the bass aria at an octave or more above the given line should also work well. If you are a tenor, singing in the soprano's key but an octave lower or a step up from that should work for you. A tenor will probably want to begin the bass aria at least a step or two higher than the bass key given. In all cases, begin with keys that place the highest note of the vocalization at a point just below the transition to the upper range.

EXERCISE

In figure 8.6, the four note functions within a musical line are labeled with either *pu* (pick-up), *fr* (framework), *c* (connector), or *te* (tapered ending). The stable singer's body serves consistent resonance throughout. Measure numbers are placed above the excerpts.

Figure 8.6.   "I know that my Redeemer liveth" (*Messiah* excerpt).

- Prepare the singer's body for good breath management and a resonant tone. Maintain the lift of the body as you begin to sing.
- The pick-up is important but must not have emphasis. It should begin gently with a mini-*crescendo* (<) that leads the listener to the next note, a framework note, as appropriate for the meter, text, and harmony.
- The skip up of a fourth requires an extra lift of the body to prevent the larynx from rising, without which vocal strain would begin.
- The semivowel [n] should provide a *legato* bridge between the first and second pitches of the phrase. Sing through it without undue tension behind the lifted tongue in the back of the mouth, the point of air restriction. As you approach the upper note, give the pitch rich resonance on the initial [n], but move into the vowel quickly after that. The [o] sound in know may need to be loosened slightly (modified) in the female voice. For the male voice, an unmodified [o] should work well and be helpful for incorporating some head voice in what may be a preparatory area.

Trap: It is common when making a skip down that the body relaxes too much, causing a diminishment of core in the tone. Such a weakening of tone disturbs the *legato* line even though the skip may be done smoothly. Although there may be some relaxation in the efforts of expansion, the efforts must not be significantly released.

- Maintain the Open Body when descending to the next two notes on "that."
- Given the caution, the jaw may be relaxed for the two connectors, since they are in the middle-to-low range of the voice and are not loud.
- The two notes given to "that" should be strong connectors, with ample volume but no emphasis, giving momentum toward the first beat of m.2. Avail yourself of the pitch properties of the [ð] in "that."
- In m.2, avail yourself of the pitch properties of the [m] in "my" for a graceful entrance into that framework note. Make use of the [ɑ] space possible behind the closed lips. You may use artistic judgment here as to how much graceful emphasis should be given to this downbeat. Just as all notes that look equal are not equal, all framework notes are not equal, not even first beats of measures. You might choose slightly less stress on the word "my" than the first notes of m.1 and m.3. Such a decision is influenced by the text and other musical elements.
- The first syllable of "redeemer" is a connector. It is a weak syllable on a weak part of the measure, but, unfortunately, it is often stressed because it is the upper pitch of a substantial skip. This situation is a real test of the body to the lift needed for the unstressed lighter registration on the upper note. It is a case where the image of "drinking in the air" might be of help. Also, female voices might need to loosen the [i] formation just a bit. Depending on the starting pitch chosen, vowel modification should not be a concern for the male voice.

Trap: Don't come off the voice on "re." Sing it with core but without emphasis.

- In the framework note of m.3, the [d] appropriately provides dramatic emphasis. However, be sure that the body is not pushing or squeezing and that the resonating spaces behind the consonant are kept open, ready for freer resonance in the subsequent vowel sound [i].
- The next two notes, one eighth and one quarter, stay true to the *legato* style but maintain strength without individual emphases.
- In m.4, the first syllable of "liveth" is a framework note, but the second is a tapered ending with a mini-*decrescendo*.
- Now that you've micromanaged the phrase by thinking about the function of each note, sing through the phrase one more time concentrating on the overarching *legato* line that begins with a gentle pick-up, blooms in continuing resonance through framework notes and connectors, and ends with a gentle tapered ending.

EXERCISE

Unlike the previous music example, which primarily gives one or two notes to a single syllable, the next music example gives as many as six notes to a single syllable. Slur marks, such as the one placed over the first syllable of "people," are often put above any two or more notes on the same syllable. This is indicative of a *legato* approach for which a flowing and consistently resonant tone must not be hampered with unnecessary emphases or interruptions. Of course, some consonants stop the tone, and in this example, there are five of them: [p] [t] [k] [d] [s]. These must be executed quickly. The continually active Open Body enables the throat to instantly spring back to an open resonating space following a restrictive consonant.

In figure 8.7, measure numbers are indicated above the excerpt. Only the pick-up, framework notes, and tapered ending are marked. All the other notes are connectors. As in figure 8.6, some framework notes might better serve musicality by functioning as connectors. Those are marked with parentheses.

Singers other than basses should choose a starting pitch that will keep them in the middle range throughout. The focus should be on executing the excerpt with a *legato* line with free resonance enabled by an Open Body and Open Throat, more than on exploring the vocal range. The guidelines offered deconstruct the phrase so that the functions of each note can be absorbed and executed, but ultimately, they are to be thought of as a unit that provides shape and direction to the entire musical line.

Figure 8.7. "The people that walked in darkness" (*Messiah* **excerpt**).

- Prepare the singer's body, pausing just a moment before beginning to sing the first note.
- Maintaining the lift of the body that accompanied the inhalation, sing the pick-up as a small *crescendo* (<) rather than as an abrupt "attack." Allow pitch to resonate through the first two letters of "The." This is brief and opens to the vowel that carries the tone to the first framework note of m.1.
- In moving to the first beat of m.1, be sure that the [p] does not elicit any pushing in the body caused by a squeeze in the rib cage. The pulse for this

consonant should be felt in the abdomen, only as much as is needed to have the nonvibrating sound sufficiently heard. The energy for this might have to be a bit exaggerated, but this must be done in the abdominals without compromising the Open Body and Open Throat.

- Sing the first four notes of m.1 as a unit consisting of the framework note and three legato connectors. Do not place any emphasis on the connectors, but maintain strength and core in the tone.

Trap: If there is any loss of expansion or any hint of push on the connectors, some notes will sound accented, thereby losing some of their potential for *legato* momentum.

- Just as the first four notes in m.1 should be sung as a unit, so should the second group of four notes in that measure. As often the case, the upper note is the most likely to be accented merely because it is higher than the others. The bass, particularly, should be increasing expansion from the third beat on because he is in his preparatory area at this point, if not at the primary transition. He should be accessing some head voice here, not only because of the pitch, but because the three notes after the framework note must not be accented or louder than the framework note. Other voice types may need to consider registration adjustments here depending on the starting pitch chosen.
- Artistically speaking, the word "darkness" in m.2 should be sung as a unit of seven notes, making the note on the third beat a connector rather than a metric framework note. All connectors should contribute to a strong forward direction possibly with some dynamic swell. However, the last two notes on the word "darkness" should be tapered very delicately with a mini-*decrescendo* before taking a quick breath.
- The following pick-up on the word "that" should begin at the same dynamic level as the preceding tapered ending so that it will not be accented and will continue the *legato* connection.

Trap: It is common that singers in a situation like this will attack the pick-up note rather than glide into it even if they have made a proper tapered ending before it. Done this way, the pick-up is jarring, breaks the *legato* line, and does not give the shape intended by the meter or the text. The dynamic of the pick-up should be the dynamic of the tapered ending. In many ways, the two functions are of the same ilk, only in reverse, as ><.

- In m.3, four note units once again give the best *legato* results. Extra attention to body expansion must be given to the upward skip from the D to the G in m.3, even though it is not a high note. Some head voice might be needed here so as not to emphasize it or cause strain. Depending on the starting pitch chosen by other voice types, this part of the music example may or may not be flirting with the preparatory area. Keep in mind that because registration shifts change according to vowel and volume, the singer must be sensitive to the slightest strain caused by not going into a lighter registration. Strain not only affects the quality of tone but causes emphases and accents that are not musically motivated.

- In m.4, the first beat that would normally be a framework note is a continuation of the four notes in the previous measure. As such, it would be less than elegant to either accent or emphasize it. However, because it is such a long connector, a slight *messa di voce* on it to prepare for the tapered ending would be appropriate.
- Now that you have micromanaged this deconstructed musical line, conscious of the different functions, go back and sing it again, with a view toward the overarching direction of the entire line. Make sure the Open Body and Open Throat are stable but flexible. The pick-ups, connectors, and tapered endings should not "come off the voice" but rather all be sung with the singer's body actively enabling consistently free resonance with Forward Articulation.

The correct functionality of notes within a musical line and registration flexibility are crucial skills for *legato* singing, especially so for melismatic and rapid passage work. Judicious use of these skills enables facility with music in which many notes are allotted to one syllable, often in rapid succession.

FAST PASSAGE WORK

The bass aria example from *Messiah* allots more than one or two notes to a single syllable in a slow tempo. Fast passage work sets many notes to a single syllable and moves at a fast pace. This style is known as *fioritura* or *coloratura*. It requires great flexibility, particularly of the vocal folds and surrounding laryngeal areas.

As discussed in earlier chapters, the size and shape of the vocal folds must change for each pitch being sung. In *fioritura*, such adjustments must be made very quickly to accommodate multitudinous pitches in a small time frame. Such a line may cover a wide range, often with skips both large and small.

The ability to execute fast passage work is relatively easy for some singers but difficult for others. Similar to the skills of singing *legato*, *fioritura* depends primarily on skill with breath management and registration. It also requires musicality that is implicit in *legato* singing. Many of the technical considerations for singing in a *legato* style are the same as for singing in a *fioritura* style.

The somewhat short *fioritura* discussion here is limited to the *legato* style, although highly accented bravura is certainly required in rage arias, drinking songs, or songs of war. In these situations, *fioritura* might be punctuated and accented with abdominal pulsing, sometimes accompanied with a slight aspirate [h] in front of every note. This is a matter of taste and style but would be indefensible in *legato* singing.

Just as in *legato* singing, the *fioritura* style includes pick-ups, framework notes, connectors, and tapered endings. Long lines of multitudinous notes in fast tempi must be executed with unhampered resonance from one fleeting note to the next. Flexible registration adjustments are important for all notes but particularly so in stepwise ascent, upward skips, or on connectors that should not be stressed. The primary difference between *fioritura* singing and any other singing is the degree of flexibility and speed with which the adjustments are made. The intricate actions of the vocal folds and surrounding structures must be served by the Open Body as well as appropriate registration choices.

To achieve greater flexibility and speed in *fioritura* singing, there must be fewer emphases (framework notes) that could weigh down the musical movement. There are fewer words in *fioritura* music, and one syllable may be extended through a string of many notes, thereby increasing the proportion of connectors. They must be lighter (not thinner) than connectors in a piece like the bass aria from the *Messiah*, for instance, which moves in a slow plodding tempo.

While the Three Steps are common denominators of all good singing, *fioritura* requires a particularly high level of finesse with breath management to enable the lighter mechanism. The reason is that any excess air pressure put on the vocal folds results in the folds bulking and becoming resistant rather than flexible, and this is antithetical to the head voice needed in the *fioritura* style. Therefore, singers are often taught to lower the volume to encourage more head voice when approaching a line of music in this style.

EXERCISE

The next two rudimentary figures show the contrast in functions between a slow vocalise and a faster one with the same pitches.

Figure 8.8. Note functions in slow vocalise.

In figure 8.8, in a rather slow tempo, the framework notes, connectors, and tapered ending function as one might expect in a 4/4 meter. They are so marked. Since the upper pitches in each pair of notes are connectors, they must be approached with a lift of the body to enable a lighter mechanism without emphasis or strain.

- Sing this vocalise with the singer's body, keeping in mind the issues of registration and function that shape the melodic line.

EXERCISE

In the following vocalise, the pitch pattern and harmonic movement of figure 8.8 is unchanged, but there are more notes per beat. The result is fewer framework notes and more connectors.

Figure 8.9.   Note functions in fast vocalise.

In figure 8.9, only the pick-up, framework, and tapered ending notes are marked. The rest are connectors. Although figures 8.8 and 8.9 have the same number of notes and the same metronome marking, there are only two framework notes in figure 8.9, as compared to five in figure 8.8. Substituting a connector for a framework note in the second beat of m.1 is admittedly an artistic decision, but this would be a typical choice for a *fioritura* line, especially at faster tempi, so as not to weigh down the musical movement or overarching shape.

- Prepare the singer's body and throat.
- Choose a pitch that will place it comfortably in your middle range. Begin in a moderate or slow tempo before trying faster tempos.
- Although the vocalise looks simple, each of the upward skips requires a lighter registration. A stable Open Body is essential to free the vocal folds to make the multiregistration adjustments needed for the *fioritura* style. (Remember that head voice, the light mechanism, often feels/sounds darker rather than thinner.) You may recall that a tendency in any ascending pitch is for the larynx to rise. This creates strain and hinders a lighter adjustment. Keeping the larynx low, primarily by means of the Open Body and Open Throat, will give the best results. The lighter registration does not necessarily imply less volume, although that certainly could assist *fioritura* lines.
- If you are not experiencing the lighter registration on the upper notes, singing those pitches on a darker [o] or [u] should help. Once you find the lighter adjustment, replace the [o] or [u] with an [a] but keep the lighter, richer quality.
- Depending on what pitch you chose, determine if you are anywhere near a preparatory area. If so, your access to head voice will be critical. However, all voices singing this kind of line must access some head voice on the upper pitches if a *legato* line is to be maintained throughout.

- As you go up the scale and increase the energy of the out-and-up pull, you must also drop the jaw more, especially on pitches that come close to your upper range. It is also important to keep whatever vowel you are singing in a vertical framework with a lowered diaphragm, comfortably low larynx, dropped jaw, and vertical mouth opening.
- Take this vocalise up by half steps, increasing the body's expansion as you go.
- As you near a transition, especially toward the upper range, you will have to increase your efforts of expansion still more.
- When you feel that you are experiencing lighter registration adjustments without losing the quality of resonance or forward motion, you may attempt to do this vocalise at progressively faster tempos. Although the pitches are changing more and more rapidly, the body must stay still and stable. Only go as fast as you are able to maintain clarity, *legato*, pitch, and rhythm—all with vocal ease. (The body will bear the workload but always with an opening sensation, not a squeezing one. Be sure that the energy is an out-and-up direction, not an in-and-down direction. The latter will inhibit adjustments.) You cannot directly control the changing adjustments of the vocal folds; you can only remove any inhibitory force from them.

Registration adjustments in the *fioritura* style can best be achieved with a stable but flexible out-and-up energy in the body. The throat must maintain its flexible open position so that fast-moving connectors are sung in a lighter registration, not a smaller resonating instrument. Volume may be lessened but with no lessening of resonance.

All fast passage work should be learned and practiced *slowly* before taking it up to tempo. Unless singing *fioritura* comes naturally to you, this is the only way to gain awareness of the particular challenges involved and to strategize for ways of meeting them. The challenges might involve issues of pitch, registration, volume, melodic contour, and/or vowels. However, when practicing in a slower tempo, use the lighter adjustments that will be needed for the embellishing connectors at the faster tempo.

Although the physiological elements of singing *fioritura* are complex and often beyond the singer's direct control, the skills of *fioritura* can be achieved through the conscious control of the body, throat, and articulators. If a singer relies on the Three Steps, at least half the work of *fioritura* is done.

EXERCISE

The vocalises of figures 8.8 and 8.9 involved small skips. Fast passage work often moves stepwise.

Figure 8.10.   Note functions in fast stepwise motion.

In many ways, the stepwise vocalise in figure 8.10 is more challenging than the previous one because the adjustments needed from step to step are minuscule compared to skips. Often the tendency is to push the registers up rather than adjust them at each step. Each pitch must open itself up to more and more head voice, lighter adjustment. While this can seem terribly detailed and difficult to accomplish, it must be remembered that the extra attention to the Open Body/Open Throat will enable these changes to occur almost naturally. Speed will not come if there is any push in the body. Too many emphasized notes also tend to slow down the movement. Think in multi-note units rather than individual notes, especially for connectors.

- Prepare the singer's body and throat. Choose a starting pitch that is comfortable and keeps you in your middle range.
- Sing this vocalise on a vowel of your choice, adding extra lift to the body as you begin the ascent and increasing the lift toward the top.
- Sing the vocalise in a slow-to-moderate tempo at first so that you can assess the needs of each note in the line.
- If you are a male and finding that the lighter adjustment is difficult for you, you might want to begin with [a] and move to [o] or [u] in ascent, maybe only at the top note at first. As you ascend further, you might want to change earlier than the top note. The female could use the same strategy, but as she nears the secondary transition, she must open more, moving all vowels closer to [a].
- Once you have found the lighter adjustment with rich tones, try using just the [a] but rounding it a little as you ascend, creating a darker vowel and concentrating on the out-and-up pull of the body and the deeper jaw drop.
- Although the framework notes receive emphasis, they never should be punched. Like the other notes, the framework notes belong to the entire continuous vocal line and should meld with it.
- Repeat the vocalise throughout the range, going faster and faster, but only go as fast as you are able to maintain clarity, *legato*, pitch, and rhythm.
- Eventually, sing the exercise with all vowel combinations to learn how different vowels function in the same context.
- As you gain enough speed, you may realize that all but the first note in each measure can function as connectors, creating the *effect* of one beat per measure. Exactly how many framework notes there are depends on the shape of the melodic line as well as the harmonic movement, so this example is only one of many ways of approaching a *fioritura* line of music.

EXERCISE

Before moving on, sing the triplets in the following vocalise. It is short but should highlight any problems you might experience as you take it up the scale. All of the guidelines given for the earlier vocalises apply to this one.

Figure 8.11.   Fast triplets.

- Prepare the singer's body and choose a starting pitch and vowel.
- Sing the vocalise of figure 8.11a at a slow-to-moderate speed at first so that you can identify the notes that will need lighter adjustments. Minimize or prevent emphasis on the third beat in favor of a strong connector and longer note units. Increasing the efforts of inhalation help with this and enable a *legato* line.
- Take the vocalise up the scale by half steps and increase the tempo as you feel secure in managing the vocalise with ease and consistent resonance.
- If you're still having trouble with adjusting toward more head voice as you ascend, alternate the [a] with [o] or [u] as in figure 8.11b. Eventually take those assists out and sing the whole line on [a], modifying as needed.
- Experiment with different vowels. Keep all vowels in a vertical framework.

These vocalises are short controlled examples that serve as an introduction to the principles of singing *fioritura*. In actual music, of course, the musical lines can become much longer and more complex. However, the principles behind the execution remain the same.

SUMMARY

The given music examples have been deconstructed to reveal how the various functions of notes in a melodic line affect the *legato* style and, in turn, the *fioritura* style. Ultimately, all notes must drive the momentum of the musical line forward and give shape to the musical line. Without that, the line is no more than black dots on a staff. Giving the musical line life is achieved largely through flexible dynamics, assisted with proper registration adjustments. The emphases of framework notes highlight the drama of text, melody, rhythm, and harmony. Connectors create a strong sense of forward direction, never letting up until the line is completed. Beginnings and endings are graceful introductions and farewells to the phrases. These elements build *legato* and empower musicality. Consistent resonance is the vehicle for it, and if one note falls out of line, the sense of direction will be momentarily lost or at least weakened. This is where the Open Body, Open Throat, and Forward Articulation must prevail. *Each of these basic elements and their relationship to one another must remain consistent but flexible throughout the entire phrase, including pick-ups, framework notes, connectors, and tapered endings.*

The functional role of individual notes in *legato* singing contributes greatly to an overarching musical line. They might be considered the microelements of the line. At a slightly more macrolevel, dynamics also contribute to the line. Changes of volume spanning a phrase ensure cohesiveness of the phrase and indicate what is most important in it. A dynamic arc can take many forms, peaking at the middle, center, or end of a phrase, depending on the musical material at hand. Like the artistic choices involved with assessing note functions, the shapes of dynamic arcs are often a matter of personal choice and taste.

The music examples offered here and the issues that they present are only a small sampling, but the principles involved in singing them with *legato* are essential to a good vocal technique as well as fine musicality. The Three Steps as enablers of good vocal technique are relevant to all forms and styles of singing. Of course, variations in performance practices, genre, and period of music all contribute to the final product, but the relationship between *legato* and musicality, also to *fioritura*, is achieved through the kinesthetic experience of the Open Body, Open Throat, and Forward Articulation.

Throughout the layering of the initial Three Steps and the refinements that followed, the OOFing mantra has retained its relevance. This is so because the trio of the Open Body, Open Throat, and Forward Articulation speaks directly to the essentials of beautiful singing, fine breath management, resonance, and enunciation. They are universal elements of all effective methods and, to my mind, are indisputable. Focusing on the kinesthetic experience involved with each step sheds light on the relationship between the body as the musical instrument and tone, as the product of that instrument. Fine singing is a product of a well-managed vocal instrument. Making a beautiful tone is an exhilarating experience for the singer and listener. It is the experience of harmony between the body and mind that creates the musical instrument that is voice.

Postlude: What Goes Around Comes Around

The Essentials of Beautiful Singing: A Three-Step Kinesthetic Approach focuses on good breath management, resonance, and enunciation as indisputable elements of fine singing technique. From beginning to end, the OOFing mantra—Open Body, Open Throat, and Forward Articulation—offers physical focal points for the singer to clarify the nature and process of developing good singing technique. The mantra "goes around" in the first offerings of part I, more so in part II, and "comes around" again and again in part III with new insights and applications.

Approaches to singing vary from teacher to teacher, singer to singer. The eight chapters in this book detail a specific and personal approach based on the following tenets: first, that the foundation of all good singing technique is centered on skills of breath management, resonance, and enunciation; second, that the applied art of singing is understood experientially and is most clearly communicated in the simplest and most specific terms possible; and, finally, that skills enabling good vocal technique are enabled by the correct kinesthetic experiences of the Open Body, Open Throat, and Forward Articulation, the physicality of the musical instrument that is the voice.

The voice is a unique and remarkable instrument. Even instrumental musicians want their instruments to "sing." Because the inner workings of the voice are indeed complex, it is understandable that the process of singing can become frustratingly mysterious to singers in training. The Three-Step Approach seeks to take much of the mystery out of fine singing. Its simplicity is extracted from physiologic and acoustic complexities largely by deconstructing them and reframing them. The approach is designed to keep the singer's eye on the ball, so to speak. The topics chosen and the exercises that flesh them out were selected because of their potential to "cut to the chase" of specific aspects of vocal technique. They are neither comprehensive nor exclusive, but I believe they are relevant and significant.

As I said in the introduction, singing and teaching singing only come alive in the "doing" of it, far beyond the "talking about it." However, both are present in this book, and both guide the singer to the "doing" part. At times, I'm sure the mindfulness required in moving through the exercises seemed painstakingly slow. I remind you here of the insight gained by my undergraduate student when she discovered that the slower she worked, the faster the results occurred.

I can only hope that, taken in its totality, the perspective of the Three-Step Approach will be of practical use to both singer and teacher of singing. It would give me great satisfaction to know that it might resonate with readers and shed some light on this path to beautiful singing.

While beautiful singing is not a one-day project, it is within the reach of all aspiring singers, from those just beginning to those who already have a good deal of experience and training. It is a process in which tangible results can and should be felt and heard at every practice session, every lesson. In this alone there is joy.

Understanding the processes of singing in meaningful and accessible ways enlightens the use of the vocal instrument. At every clarifying step along the way, the well-trained singer gains greater and greater freedom for artistic expression. In this process, the singer discovers a voice not only literally but metaphorically as well. This is the reason why students of singing have such great passion for their art and why teachers of singing find so much reward in the role they play. It has certainly fueled my enthusiasm for teaching for more than thirty years.

Just as I have always welcomed and appreciated interaction with singers and teachers, I invite readers of this book to share with me their comments and questions regarding the Three-Step Approach. Teachers and singers are enriched by pooling their information and perspective with others invested in beautiful singing. It is good for students to be part of this dialogue, too, sometimes in affirmation of a particular element of technique, sometimes with challenge. Both are good! Students need to learn how to assess varying approaches as they go out in the world and on to other voice studios, other coaches. We as teachers must prepare them for making assessments of those encounters, for they are often defining factors in their professional life.

Finally, I offer my gratitude for the voice teachers I've met, the clinicians of the master classes I've attended, and the authors whose works have inspired me. These provided many opportunities to expand my horizons, and they have contributed in one way or another to the personal perspective on voice teaching shared in this book. I also feel fortunate to have worked with many wonderful students who brought their enthusiasm, hard work, passion, and commitment to my studio. My responsibility was to teach them, and their responsibility was to learn, and in that we shared much. They have been my source of inspiration in the voice studio, in voice pedagogy class, and in the process of writing this book!

Appendix: Selected International Phonetic Alphabet Symbols and Corresponding English Words

Vowels	Words	Consonants	Words
[ɑ]	father, water	[b]	bat, able
[e]	babe	[d]	dad, sending
[i]	see, tea	[f]	fat, fluff
[o]	low, so	[g]	got, leg
[u]	too, suit	[h]	hot, help
[æ]	sat, back	[j]	yet, yam
[ɛ]	bet, next	[k]	kit, cap
[ɪ]	sit, bitter	[l]	late, halt
[ɔ]	caught, saw	[m]	man, woman
[ʌ]	but, muffle	[n]	now, tin
[ʊ]	foot	[p]	paper, pop
		[r]	rat, rise
		[s]	some, toss
		[t]	torn, went
		[v]	very, wave
		[w]	wave, west
		[z]	zebra, jazz
		[ʒ]	azure, leisure
		[dʒ]	jump, fudge
		[ŋ]	rung, sing
		[ʃ]	shut, hush
		[tʃ]	church, saturate
		[θ]	thick, wrath
		[ð]	then, writhe
		[hw]	why, what
		[ks]	ax, ticks

Index

abdominals, 12, 14, 18, 21, 24, 25, 26, 27, 38, 113, 114, 118, 134. *See also* posture
abdominal tuck, 14
Adam's apple, 32, 49
air flow, 28, 32, 35, 36, 39
Alexander technique, 9, 36
alignment. *See* posture
appoggio, 24. *See also* exhalation for singing
arpeggio, 111, 115
articulation, 55–73
articulators, 55, 61; jaw, 27, 37, 38, 52, 58, 62–64, 86, 107; lips, 58–59, 61; mouth, 3, 33–34, 44, 45, 47–48, 52, 67, 68; soft palate, 46, 49–51, 61, 93, 97; tongue, 34, 42, 47, 52–53, 59, 61, 62, 64–66, 93

bel canto, 32
blends. *See under* registers
breath control, 18, 36
breath flow, 26
breath management, 17–29
breath "support," 18
bright/dark. *See chiaroscuro*

cavities, air-filled, 3, 5, 21, 31, 33–35, 37. *See also* resonance
chest voice. *See under* registers
chest register in female voice, 82–92
chiaroscuro, 48, 55, 66–73, 93, 122
clutching of soft palate, 50–51.
coloratura. See fast passage work
connector. *See under* note functions
consciousness raising, 37–38, 39, 41, 85
consonants, 44, 60–61, 126, 132. *See also* articulation
cover, 94

dark/bright. *See chiaroscuro*
diaphragm, 19–22, 29, 38, 49, 113
down-out-and-up. *See under* inhalation
"drinking in the air," 112. *See also* inhalation

efforts of expansion. *See under* inhalation
energy, 18, 22, 24, 107
enunciation. *See* articulation
exhalation for singing, 19, 23–29. *See also* breath management
expansion of thorax, 26, 29, 36, 37, 38

falsetto, 92
fast passage work, 134–139
fioritura. See fast passage work
folds, vocal. *See* vocal folds
forward/back. *See under* placing the voice
forward placement. *See* placing the voice
framework notes. *See under* note functions
frequency, 33

glottal attack, 50

head voice. *See under* registers
heavy register. *See under* registers
humming, 43

imagery and singing, xvi–xvii, 47
in-and-down muscles. *See under* inhalation
inhalation, 19–22; down-out-and-up muscles of, 20, 29, 39, 87, 107, 108, 137; efforts of expansion/inhalation, 23, 26, 29, 43, 87, 94, 107, 129; in-and-down muscles, 22, 106, 108, 118, 119, 122, 165; out-and-up muscles, 29, 39, 87, 107, 108, 137. *See also* breath management

About the Author

Dr. Karen Tillotson Bauer is professor of music, head of the voice department, and director of the master of music in vocal performance at North Park University, Chicago, Illinois, where she has taught voice and voice pedagogy for over thirty years. She has distinguished herself as an effective pedagogue whose former students have been successful in establishing professional careers in teaching and performance. At North Park, inspired by her earlier opera studies under Boris Goldovsky and Robert Gay, she has directed the Opera Workshop. She has staged opera scenes for the Opera Festival di Roma, Italy, where she also taught voice. Having sung in professional ensembles under the direction of Robert Shaw, Leonard Slatkin, Georg Solti, Carlo Maria Giulini, and many other international conductors, she conducted the North Park Chamber Singers for several years and toured with them in the United States and South Korea. She was invited back to Korea for a tour of master classes on vocal techniques for the solo singer. Bauer has presented numerous master classes in the states and abroad, most currently for undergraduates and graduates in vocal performance at the University of London, England. Bauer's two-part article on the Baroque Solo Cantata, published in 2007 by the National Association of Teachers of Singing's *Journal of Singing*, offered a comprehensive analysis of three cantatas by Vivaldi, Bach, and Handel as a reference for the solo singer. A longtime member of the National Association of Teachers of Singing, Bauer is a former president of the Chicago chapter. Her passion for teaching professionally bound singers and training effective voice teachers led to her unique three-step approach, which gives fresh insight and remarkable clarity to the process of singing as it is experienced by the singer and communicated by the teacher.